MANAGING A SHOOT

MANAGING
A SHOOT

M.I.L. ROBERTS

° THE °
SPORTSMAN'S
PRESS
LONDON

Published by The Sportsman's Press, 1990

For my daughters,
Georgina and Harriet

British Library Cataloguing in Publication Data
Roberts, M. I. L.
Managing a shoot.
1. Great Britain. Game birds. Shoots. Management
I. Title

ISBN 0–948253–43–6

Photoset and printed in Great Britain
by Redwood Press Limited, Melksham, Wiltshire

Contents

List of Illustrations

Acknowledgements

The author would like to thank the following for permission to reproduce photographs:

F. P. B. J. Roosendaal: Plates 1, 3, 4, 5 (below), 6, 7, 8 (above), 9, 10, 11

Peter Collins: Plates 2, 5 (above), 8 (below), 12 (above)

B. Culley: Plate 12 (below)

Foreword

Managing a shoot is something into which most people stumble by chance. Some are pushed by so-called friends, others deliberately 'take up the White man's burden'.

No matter how they got involved, few get through their first season without qualms about taking on the commitment. If *they* don't, their matrimonial partners certainly do! Struggling to keep business activities on an even keel, and social life and marriage off the rocks, the first time shoot manager gets a nasty shock. He suddenly realises that running a shoot in what is laughingly called spare time, is actually a bigger and more complex operation than the full time work of some friends. Big shoots represent big pressures; smaller shoots are no guarantee of an easy ride. When things go wrong with birds, staff, weather, vehicles, vermin or whatever, the experience can be bruising. On the brighter side when things go right, managing a shoot can be stimulating, rewarding and very good fun indeed.

Most of this book concentrates on managing pheasant shoots. No excuses are made for this bias towards the phasian bird. No one can deny that the pheasant is the dominant game bird of the British countryside. Heather moors and tidal marshes apart, he is often the only game bird around. Pheasants thrive in a changing agricultural landscape that has all but seen off the grey partridge. Pheasants are relatively easy to breed; properly presented, they fly high and fast; on the dinner table they compare favourably with the best. What more can you ask of a game bird?

Having said all that, the management and presentation of other game species is not ignored. These may represent a minority of the bag but they add interest, variety and zest to a day's sport. Partridge, grouse, blackgame, capercaillie, snipe, woodcock, duck, geese, hares and pigeons all get a mention.

A new shoot manager must, at the earliest opportunity, thoroughly understand his land from a game presentation and conservation point of view. This is very different from knowing the place as a farmer, or as a forester. It is also different from the view of a guest or syndicate gun, standing at the receiving end of a drive.

Most birds and animals are creatures of fixed habits. A shoot manager has to learn how his birds react to ground and weather conditions, know the preferred roosting areas in different parts of the shoot, how particular groups of birds travel, where they feed, and where they just loiter about. He must know which way birds are prepared to be driven, and equally important, which ways they will not be pushed under any circumstances.

The initial purpose of this book was to make life easier and more enjoyable for the new shoot manager in his first season or two. The outcome is a book which could, with advantage, be read by all game shooters and all who work gun dogs. Being part of a well run day's shooting is a pleasant and congenial experience; however, like watching ice dancing or good skiing, it is all too easily taken for granted. Knowledge of the hard graft and professionalism that produces a skilled performance, helps appreciation of excellence as and when it is encountered.

'Old sweat' shoot managers will probably learn little from reading this book. They may, however, be reminded of hard and uncomfortable lessons learned in the past, and *almost* forgotten.

1 : How Much Shooting?

How much shooting will the land support? This the first, foremost and fundamental question to be addressed by any prospective shoot manager. It is not an
easy one to answer.

Most tracts of countryside have a potential to support some wild game. Travel
through parts of France or Southern Ireland where organised game shooting is
long gone, and it soon becomes apparent just how small that potential can be. Not
dissimilar countryside in Southern England appears to be walking with game.
The difference between the two scenarios is what game conservation and game
shooting is all about.

Partridge and grouse, pheasant and hares all tend to be highly visible in the
countryside; they also look good to eat. This fact does not go unnoticed by a legion
of feathered and four-legged predators and by man himself. Only when such
predators are controlled and constrained is a shootable surplus of one species
generated.

In parts of continental Europe, game birds face depredation from an unusual
predator – wild boar. These bristly characters do not often catch adult birds; what
they do with great proficiency is find the nests of ground nesting birds and eat the
eggs. Those highly sensitive porcine noses, which enables domestic pigs to be
trained as truffle hunters, are equally adept at finding piggy delicacies – fresh
eggs. A sitting pheasant or partridge has a good chance of being undetected by fox
or badger but little chance of escaping the attention of wild boar. Very few wild
bred pheasants occur in boar-infested forests.

Geography, local climate, soil type, farming practices and the nature and
pattern of woodlands, reed bed and other cover, all influence the ability of
country to attract and hold wild game. The relationship of one block of country to
its neighbour is also of great importance. Fifty acres of woodland in the middle of
a treeless arable prairie clearly has more potential to hold game than when
surrounded by woods of similar size and composition.

Since hunting with hounds and subsequently game shooting took over from
falconry as the great field sports of this country, woodland and forests have often
been planted with more than half an eye to their sporting potential. A few
hundred years later the land sometimes ends up in unappreciative hands. The
hunting man is heard to grumble that foxes really don't like those steep hanging

woods along his valley. The shooting man finds it difficult to move pheasants out of those dense woodland thickets in the valley bottom. Each has sporting rights over land tailored to the needs of the other. No doubt in the fullness of time, the sporting wheel turns a full circle and all can then be happy.

Any tract of countryside is constantly changing as is its shooting potential. Woods are planted, grow up, are thinned and eventually felled. Brambles and bushwood can appear and choke an area in a very few years. Local crop patterns and the available wild food supply can change for better or for worse. The water table can rise or fall, lakes, ponds and marshy areas come and go. New roads, new houses and barn conversions impinge on wilderness areas.

On some long-established shoots this constant process of metamorphosis is ignored. Woods are driven today in exactly the same way as in grandfather's time, but the woodland and other conditions are not the same as those which faced grandfather and his pheasants. Obviously some birds still fly reasonably well or such drives would be scrapped. As in school reports however, 'could do better' is often an appropriate comment. Badgers may continue to use an ancestral sett long after forests have been cut down, and the place has reverted to parkland or meadow. Game birds and ground game react to the more immediate conditions of here and now. If they don't like them, they tend to move off – regardless of blandishments.

Steps can of course be taken to improve the game holding potential of land, and make it perform better, or sooner than would otherwise be the case. By the same token, steps can be taken to slow down the erosion and steady losses of game habitat – as by the relentless growth of pine trees in large numbers.

On easy land with natural advantages, game need not be expensive to preserve and shoot. On difficult land with few natural advantages, such activities will always be more expensive. When in doubt as to what level of shooting your land will support, aim to understock and perhaps undershoot, rather than go to extremes.

Always remember that 'tuning up' a shoot takes time and costs money. Beware of falling into the trap of thinking that, with enough cash and effort, all shoot-related problems can be overcome. A 'sow's ear' of a shoot can only be changed into a better 'sow's ear', no matter what you spend. Conversly even the best 'silk purse' of a shoot can be worn out and destroyed by excess and abuse.

When the nature of a tract of countryside changes fundamentally, so too must its sporting use. As partridge stocks declined in the early years of this century, a number of great partridge manors switched to pheasants. Purists wrung their collective hands in despair – this was clearly a dastardly and retrograde step. But two generations of sportsmen later, a considerable number of those very estates still have first class shoots. They were right to change when circumstances altered.

So – how much shooting *will* the land support? It is an undeniable fact that the depth of financial pockets of those concerned, and how deeply people are pre-pared to dig, gives part of the answer. It is also undeniable that the true cost – and here one must emphasise the word *true* – per pheasant, partridge, grouse or whatever shot, varies dramatically from shoot to shoot. The more highly tuned a shoot becomes, the higher tends to become the cost per bird shot.

For most people the amount of shooting their land will support is a factor of what can be achieved at a realistic price. For this reason alone, the value-for-money aspect of shoot management is a recurring theme in this book.

2 : Gamekeepers

Reviewing the year ahead, a shoot manager is not unlike a man about to build his own house: both have clear objectives; both have financial constraints; both are confronted by a range of options.

At an early stage, the housebuilder has to decide how best to undertake basic excavations, and get the footings dug. Does he take a spade and do it himself? Does he employ ten navvies with larger spades? Does he call in a contractor with earth-moving machinery? Balancing time, cost and convenience of each alternative, is what management is all about.

At a very early stage, shoot managers must resolve the gamekeeper problem. In grandfather's day, three keepers, each with two boys, were employed on the estate. Today a single keeper handles an even bigger shoot. In grandfather's day, twenty men and as many horses farmed the land. Another gang of men worked full time in the woods. Those in the saw mill produced fence posts, gates and hurdles; others worked pruning and thinning trees, cutting undergrowth, clearing storm damage and providing waggon loads of firewood for the big house and for estate workers. Today the land is farmed by three men. One of them works part time in the woods.

In living memory not only farming and forestry, but gamekeeping as well, have swung from labour intensive to capital intensive activities. Farm workers and foresters now have more mechanical power and chemical wizzardry to their elbows than was dreamed of a century ago. Gamekeepers, too, have more equipment and resources than ever before.

Time was when a gamekeeper's needs were simple. A gun, some gin traps, chicken coops, poison for crows, wire for snares, two bicycles, and he was in business. Two bikes rather than one were necessary to counter local poachers. The system worked like this: the bikes were ridden turn and turnabout; at most times of day and sometimes at night, a keeper's bike would be seen propped up and highly visible somewhere around the estate. Everyone knew he had two bikes, but at any given time it was impossible to tell which bike was in use and which was the decoy. Accordingly, you could never be sure where the old keeper was lurking. This game of cat and mouse kept local poachers on their toes and saved many pheasants from an untimely end.

Today's gamekeeper demands, and usually gets, lots of equipment and back-up resources: laying pens, release pens, catchers, incubators, gas or electric brooders, feed hoppers, a cupboard full of medications, poisons and chemical sprays, and goodness knows what else. By the time a newly appointed man puts on his keepersuit, takes down a gun and climbs into a vehicle – all supplied by the shoot – he has usually demonstrated just how capital intensive the job has become.

But expense does not end there: gamekeepers have to be housed. That bicycle-riding predecessor lived in a rudimentary cottage, close to the wood, and up a desperately muddy lane. Because the nearest metalled road was a mile away, the keeper's family kept their better boots and shoes in a box hidden in the roadside hedge. When children went to school or the keeper's wife went shopping, they changed boots at the box and walked into town relatively cleanly shod. On the return journey, the cleaner boots went back into the box, prior to the last muddy trudge home.

The house of most modern keepers is vastly different. It probably has a tame rabbit living with assorted dogs in the kitchen, ferrets in the spare bedroom and a one-legged pink footed goose in the garden. In all other respects it is a desirable rural residence. So desirable in fact, that, were a keeper not in residence, affluent town dwellers would run barefoot over hot bricks to buy the place for a remarkable sum of money.

If he wanted to show pheasants or partridge in decent numbers, the old time keeper had to plan his programme well in advance. Stock birds had to be caught-up, eggs produced, broody hens scrounged from miles around, sitting birds tended, rearing field set up, and so on. The modern keeper has access to an army of support services. Game farmers, feed compounders and equipment suppliers vie with each other to provide birds, feed stuffs and medications on what is virtually an 'instant' basis. In the case of medications, countless thousands of young birds now survive each year, firstly because modern remedies such as those for black head or gapes actually work; secondly because birds are spared the ferocious home-made cure-all medicines which old time keepers used to inflict upon their charges.

If modern gamekeepers can opt to minimise involvement with chores such as catching up stockbirds, collecting and washing eggs and the like, and still be able to put on an appropriate number of birds to covert, so too can anyone else.

Few shoot managers can afford to ignore the value for money aspects of their sport. Most are agreed that, good or bad, young or old, paragon of virtue or drunken scoundrel, all full time gamekeepers are expensive. This begs two fundamental questions: Are full-time keepers really necessary? What are the alternatives?

The second question is easier to answer than the first. Britain is extremely well endowed with potential gamekeepers. Advertise such a position and people respond from far and near. Butchers and bakers, firemen and busdrivers, policemen and accountants, plus of course some existing gamekeepers – all want to be considered. Most amateurs seeking to turn professional know quite a lot about shooting; whether as beaters, pickers-up or shoot helpers, they tend to have been on the fringes of keepering for years. The more serious prospects will appreciate that keepering is not well paid and lacks the holidays and fringe benefits which are often taken for granted in urban work.

Some of the amateurs who apply for keeping work are little more than starry-eyed idealists. They feel it would be a great life to walk around the countryside all day with a dog and gun, which is of course, all that keepers do! The 'old sweat' keeper, with polished leather boots, who applies for the job, has probably been a professional for longer than his interviewer has been shooting. This man has a good interview manner, an old world politeness and talks freely on all aspects of keepering. There are plausible reasons for some gaps in his working career and for occasional terms of unemployment; 'the old squire was killed out hunting', 'the estate was sold', 'a new motorway ruined the main coverts and the syndicate disbanded' and so on. The wife of the 'old sweat' keeper is clean and polite and looks the part. You may be tempted to give them a try but be very, very, careful. This sort of keeper has probably forgotten more ways of taking employers for a ride and lining his own pockets than most of his interviewers ever knew existed.

If you want and need a full-time keeper, amateur applicants can and should be given serious consideration. If they are married, however, it is absolutely essential to meet and talk with the wife. He may know exactly what he is letting himself in for: solitary and often demanding work, in all weathers. She may never have lived away from an urban community. She doesn't beat, pick-up or join her husband when he works on the shoot. The full reality of living off the beaten track as a keeper's wife may not be appreciated. It must be, if an appointment is to be successful and lasting.

For every aspiring full-time keeper, there are many other shoot enthusiasts and helpers who will not, or cannot, give up existing employment. This however does not stop them spending long hours – evenings, weekends and holidays – beavering away on the shoot. Given the support of the shoot manager, perks and some pocket money, the workload with which one or two such individuals can cope with is quite extraordinary.

Here then is the alternative to a full-time keeper; part-time shoot helpers. So, are full-time keepers really necessary?

Each case must be studied on its own merits. In broad terms, if you aspire to shoot over 3000 birds a year you need a full-time keeper. If you expect to shoot less than 1000 birds a year, you probably don't need a full time keeper. In between these numbers you have to do some value-for-money arithmetic. The true cost per bird shot varies more widely from shoot to shoot than many suspect (and others are prepared to admit). Costs are influenced by two groups of factors; some the shoot manager can control or influence, others he cannot.

Factors which lend themselves to lower cost shooting and therefore mitigate in favour of part-time keepering are:

- Patterns of agriculture and forestry which make for 'game friendly' land, i.e., warm woods, natural food supplies.
- Shooting which is not highly tuned in terms of birds per acceptable acre of land.
- Minimal public access by roads, trackways or footpaths.
- Landowners and local farmers who are friendly and helpful.
- Some organised game conservation on adjoining land.
- Shoot manager lives on or very close to the shoot.

The more these factors relate to a particular shoot, the better its prospect of producing not too expensive shooting. Also the more likely that part-time keepering is a viable option.

The reverse is equally true. When the following set of circumstances apply, shooting is almost invariably more expensive and more troublesome to organise, so a full-time keeper is more likely to be necessary:

- Land is bleak and the composition of woodland (or its lack) makes for a non 'game friendly' environment.
- Shoot success depends on a high concentration of birds per acceptable acre of land.
- Roads and tracks crisscross the land and are heavily used by the public.
- The local climate is essentially wet.
- Poacher and predator control present difficulties.
- Locals are less than friendly towards the shoot.
- Shoot management lives too far away to keep a close eye on proceedings.

During his working year, a typical professional keeper handles between ten and twenty days of formal shooting. By comparison he spends four to five months of his time preoccupied with rearing game birds. A part-time keeper can readily handle shooting days. However, he clearly cannot do all the things which a full-time man does, especially with regard to the rearing programme. When doing the arithmetic, a shoot manager must explore the cost of self sufficiency, as compared to buying in eggs, birds, supplies or services from outside. He must also look at ways of saving costs and generating extra revenue within the game rearing situation.

Sporting agreements cover finite periods, so shoot management must ponder carefully any proposed capital expenditure; this especially for items like release pens, which cannot be removed when a sporting tenancy ends. The real secret of good shoot management is making the best possible use of available resources; these include the skills and experience of all associated with the shoot, as well as the more obvious bricks and mortar, pens, incubators, vehicles and boats. Old keepering dogs are very slow to learn new tricks – beware of brave new ideas which will involve retraining your keeper.

On a newly created shoot, or where organised shooting has lapsed for many years, the evaluation of options by the shoot manager is often much easier. For instance, if there is no keeper's cottage, and premises would need to be bought or rented in the open market, this factor alone must produce a large cash negative against appointing a full-time keeper. On the other hand, where a situation is marginal, and the existing keeper's cottage is buried in the shoot alongside your best wood, this must favour retention of a keeper. No shooting manager in his right mind relinquishes control of a property, which, in unfriendly hands, could ruin the shooting.

A section on rearing game occurs later in this book, but brief comments are included here on how this affects the ongoing keepering job. The four main steps of game rearing are: egg production, incubation, rearing and release of birds. During the course of arithmetical calculations, a shoot manager must explore which of these steps to undertake on the shoot, and what to buy in from suppliers.

In the total opt-out situation, a shoot manager may decide to buy in all stock as hardened poults at ten weeks old. This is likely to be the most expensive solution, but it may make commercial sense. At the other extreme, a shoot manager may equip his keeper to do everything himself. Somewhere between the two lies the logical best solution for most shoots. Thus, if a shoot has good laying pens in a safe place where hen birds are not prone to vanishing in early April, a shoot manager may opt to produce all his own eggs. If he has a person or persons skilled at catching-up laying stock, this option is doubly attractive. Game bird eggs are the base material of inter-shoot barter arrangements; they can be swopped for day old chicks, grown poults, feedstuffs, eggs or chicks of other species, and so on.

If the shoot has recently bought a commercial incubator, it may be sensible to utilise that asset by hatching your own, or bought-in, eggs. Some additional cash can also be generated by contract hatching eggs for shooting neighbours. But here two big words of caution must be interposed: *take care*. Converting fertile eggs into chicks is a balance of electricity, time, machine performance and operator skills. Many of those splendid looking turkey incubators, tucked away in sheds behind keeper's houses, produced very variable results. These machines were usually bought secondhand by the shoot and even the original users found them difficult. Good results are too dependent upon operator skills for the peace of mind of those who foot the ultimate bill. Total disasters may not be commonplace with shoot incubators; failures tend to be hushed-up. There is no doubt however, that through minor mistakes, a lot of game birds' eggs get wasted each year.

Professional game farmers and hatcheries do this job better than most. They will typically produce 10% more live chicks than your average keeper. On 5000 or so pheasant eggs, that is a lot of extra day-old chicks available to be traded for poults, used to offset hatching costs, or put to some other good use.

The result of shoot managers' deliberations may indicate that shoot interests will be better served by one or more part-time helpers than by a full-time keeper. When this is the case, it does not necessarily mean that the present keeper incumbent should be flung out on his ear. It does mean that, when death or departure removes that man, he should not be replaced, without first making a very careful reappraisal of the facts.

The performance of one particular shoot had long been deteriorating. The ageing gamekeeper drank too much and worked too little; everyone knew this, but the old man had been around for twenty years. One day, Mother Nature and Father Time conspired, and resolved the problem once and for all. It was the middle of the shooting season and not an opportune time to recruit a successor. No one did any sums to see if a successor was indeed necessary.

The keeper's widow asked if she could stay in the cottage until the end of the season; in return she would feed the birds and trap vermin. On humanitarian rather than altruistic grounds, this was agreed. Now the keeper's widow looked unbelievably ancient, and was of fearsome appearance. The combined talents of Central Casting and the Royal Shakespeare Company would be hard pushed to find a more convincing looking old hag to stir the cauldron in the opening scene of Macbeth. There was no real doubt that she could feed the birds. Her black-shawled figure had been seen shuffling around the woods on many occasions. No one expected any vermin to be caught. They could not have been more wrong.

The old crone was absolute mustard with trap and snare. The catch would be laid out every morning at the shoot manager's back door; often there would be a note asking him to shoot a fox at such and such a place. She never carried nor would use a gun – that was man's work! With hindsight this apparent late flowering talent was easily understood; for many years the keeper's wife had done all vermin control on the place. While he lay comatose in bed at 5.00 am it was she who shuffled around the trap line, whilst he got the credit for whatever was caught. With husband out of the way the old widow caught more vermin than ever before. A farm worker took over running shooting days, shoot costs went down, results went up. The old keeper was not replaced, everyone seemed happy. For the next five years, and until the old crone rejoined her drunken husband in some other place, the shoot manager's job was remarkably easy.

Whether full-time professional or part-time amateur, three main work aspects confront the keeper:

– Rearing and holding game.
– Presenting game on shoot days.
– Controlling vermin and poachers.

Most keepers are good at one aspect, some are good at two, a very, very small minority excel at all three. The extent to which a shoot manager has an easy or a hard time, will be markedly influenced by the ability of his keeper or keepers, and by where their respective talents lie.

The keeper whose main strength is rearing is seen at his best in late summer. As usual he has had a good rearing season; fine, well grown pheasant poults are in the release pens and out on feed rides. Knowing the tendency for numbers to dwindle rather fast as autumn progresses, and predators grow more hungry, the keeper actually has more birds in the woods than his shoot manager knows (have you ever tried counting several hundred poults in a release pen?).

By the time shooting commences there is still a fair number of birds around, but on shoot days they are presented terribly. Birds fly around in all directions, and the occasional dramatic flush puts a hundred birds in a cloud over one startled gun. People get unhappy.

The keeper who is bad at rearing may be the one who excels on shoot days. Beaters are well drilled, move through the woods in a businesslike manner, sticks tap steadily and there is none of the 'tiger shoot pandemonium' which is so often evident when beaters are in woodland. 'Stops' are standing in just the right places, and what birds there are fly well but the shoot manager is worried at how few birds seem to be around. The visitors are impressed by professionalism, if disappointed by the bag. The keeper tells his shoot manager that the best is yet to come, but knows full well it has gone. A series of hatching and rearing disasters, some declared, others concealed, left this man chronically short of birds, even at the release pen stage. If he devoted just a little more time to improving his rearing techniques and controlling foxes, and less to drilling and disciplining his army of beaters, this type of keeper would not lose so many of his scarce young birds before the shooting season started.

The keeper who is predominantly a vermin and poacher man is pretty rare, but does exist. The old keeper's widow already discussed, was almost this; she would never have tackled a poacher, but her sudden appearance in bad light would have scared the wits out of most men. The old-time keeper's gibbet was an interesting but not very attractive sight and it smelt distinctly evil. Its virtual demise is only regrettable in one way: like it or not, the gibbet provided a highly visible record of just what vermin a keeper had accounted for.

Even with modern aids, today's keepers account for a fraction of the stoats, weasels, polecats, rats and assorted predators slain by their predecessors. Foxes alone, are, for the most part, quite well controlled. This is because they are large, highly visible and prompt embarrassing question when they come trotting out of the wood in mid pheasant drive; also their pelts can have value.

Like most of us, modern gamekeepers are compulsive users of motor vehicles and rarely walk if they can drive. As they speed around in van or Land Rover, they miss seeing signs which tell what predators are about, where and how they are hunting. Tracks, droppings, feathers, scratch marks, broken egg shells, traces of fur, all have a story to tell. Without that knowledge the mysterious attrition of young pheasants continues unchecked.

The effective shoot manager learns the strengths and weaknesses of his keeper at the earliest possible opportunity. If he is fortunate, his own skills and experience will complement rather than duplicate those of his keeper. For instance, by taking a very firm control of all aspects, a shoot manager can effectively 'carry' a keeper who is weak on shoot days. To achieve this the shoot manager will almost certainly have to devote much time and effort. He will probably need to walk every drive with his keeper a week ahead of that shoot, see that every gun peg is placed in exactly the right place, plastic bags or markers are put in hedgerows and wood to show precisely where each 'stop' has to stand, and where the beating line halts or turns in key manoeuvres.

Enhancing egg production or game rearing performance of a keeper is exceedingly difficult and tends to be counter productive. If the man is no good at producing eggs you have little choice but to buy them; if his rearing performance is marginal, then you are probably better off buying poults which someone else has reared. If the shoot is not viable as a result of all this buying, that particular keeper will probably have to go.

Teaching keepers how to be more effective catchers of predators is extremely difficult. The best alternative is probably to get your man to spend a few days with the gamekeeper of friends or neighbours, who is known to be strong on vermin. Teaching poacher control is also a problem; a shoot manager can lay down all sorts of criteria for patrolling at night, also keep a high profile in areas like laying and release pens where poachers may strike. He can do little to improve effectiveness, if and when that keeper actually gets into woods.

As sometimes intimated in this chapter, gamekeepers are not always paragons of virtue. Their tendency to indulge in nefarious activities is probably no greater or no less than with other groups in society. Keepers are, however, in positions of trust and for this reason it comes as a particular shock to many employers if and when they find that their keeper has been deceiving them. The great protection against employing a dishonest keeper, or one with a criminal past, is the practice of taking up references. Where the answer is favourable, past employers will usually write a formal note confirming this; when things are not good, ex-employers are usually reluctant to write anything; most, however, are prepared to talk about problems which may have occurred with a particular man. The prospective employer can then judge for himself whether such disclosures mitigate against or in favour of the man. One very able gamekeeper was rather too successful as a ladies' man and on at least one occasion he had to leave his employment or risk being lynched by a growing number of locals, whose wives or daughters had become enamoured. There was no question of his keepering ability or honesty being in doubt, but he lacked discretion. It was right, however, that a prospective employer of this man knew of his amorous past, and was able to weigh in the balance the prospect of the same thing happening again.

Everyone who employs a keeper should make the appointment subject to receipt of satisfactory references, and ensure that those references are followed up. Amazingly, this formality is frequently overlooked. In several cases known to the author, keepers dismissed for misconduct – in two cases criminal misconduct – have been back in keepering jobs within the year. None of the employers who dismissed these men was approached for either a verbal or written reference. No doubt the keepers involved spun convincing yarns why references should not be applied for. Con men in all walks of life have to be plausible and believable to be successful.

Any shoot manager who fails to take up keeper references has only himself to blame when he makes an uncomfortable and expensive mistake.

3 : Eggs and Laying Stock

Not every shoot has obvious facilities to produce game bird eggs and not every shoot manager has obvious inclinations to get embroiled in such activities, but in a sport where cash outlay constantly threatens to overwhelm income, producing game bird eggs can make financial sense.

Pheasant eggs and to a lesser extent those of partridge and wild duck, are the basic trading commodity of the game rearing industry. With the right eggs, in the right place, at the right time, scope for a shoot manager to negotiate impressive barter or whatever deals are legion.

With value for money in mind, it is fortuitous that three of our main game bird species are tolerant of flock mating. Furthermore, pheasants, red-legged partridge and mallard will, if given enough elbow room, tolerate each other's company in the same laying pen. This is not ideal, but is acceptable when circumstances so demand. Given multiple pen occupancy red-legged partridge hens tend to come out bottom of the pecking order, which may reduce the number of eggs they lay. At the other end of the spectrum it is amusing to see how a cock pheasant in sartorial splendour, with admiring wives all around, does not wait to argue when a grumpy drake mallard heads in his direction!

Laying pens were traditionally tucked away in remote corners of the shoot; this was an excellent way of keeping the birds undisturbed. Today such pens are an ideal place from which to steal birds. A hundred or so wing-clipped or brailed pheasants in a laying pen are not difficult to catch. A couple of men with a Land Rover full of bird crates, salmon landing nets and the odd spaniel, can empty the place in double quick time.

In March and April, hen pheasants are very much in demand. This is the time when keepers who have overshot their land suddenly realize they cannot possibly catch-up enough birds for their own laying pens. Usually unbeknown to their employers, keepers fund a not insignificant black market in stolen hen pheasants. On the open market, if available, such birds are suddenly worth four or five time the 'butcher's meat' value of their less fortunate sisters, who failed to survive the last shoot of the season. When no questions are asked and payment is in cash, hen birds fetch even higher prices. It is a harrowing experience, after weeks of catching-up effort, to have stock birds stolen in the night.

Villains with local knowledge or local tip offs are not the only threat to isolated laying pens. The phenomena of footpath walkers is now a fact of life in many parts of the country. Furthermore, such walkers tend to materialise miles away from designated footpaths. It is not unknown for well-meaning but misguided individuals, to open a pen and release wing-clipped or brailed birds into the woods. The ideal position for today's laying pen is quiet, but as close as possible to the dwelling of someone who can safeguard the birds.

Laying pens must not double as release pens, because of avian disease: gape worms and the like. A laying pen is therefore used for just three months of the year. It does not have to be a permanent structure and for many reasons, is perhaps best when it can be moved about.

Faced with a bird stealing crisis, the author once fenced off a small orchard at the bottom of his garden. Two children's ponies were moved out, and five hundred pheasants moved in. They were later joined by a few guinea fowl and some wild duck and they all got on extremely well. The only ones who suffered were the ponies, who did not seem to think the grass tasted too good when they later reclaimed their paddock!

Faced with the prospect of creating a new laying pen, the shoot manager should first have a good look around for ready-made solutions. Old walled kitchen gardens or disused farm yards which can be made fox proof, are obvious choices. Tennis courts can also make excellent laying pens as they tend to be in private gardens, to be surrounded by chain link fencing, and have lockable doors. Those with old-fashioned shale surfaces are especially suitable, and are also likely to be less cherished than a brand new court. If a court is tennis ball proof, then it should, in theory, prevent pheasants or other inmates getting out and predators getting in. But do check most carefully that the bottom of the netting is securely anchored. A tennis ball does not struggle too much to get out; a hungry fox or badger can be quite industrious when it wants to get in.

The actual playing surface of the chosen tennis court can be kept completely clear of pine branches for nesting cover, dust baths, feeders, drinkers and other impedimenta as there is usually plenty of room for these at the ends and sides. In mid May when an appropriate number of eggs have been collected, the tennis court can be cleared of assorted rubbish, swept, hosed down, and tennis can commence. It is surely no hardship for a shooting man's family not be able to play tennis during those chilly months of spring!

Laying pens, wherever located, are powerful magnets for egg eating birds. Even before the assembled pheasants came into lay, a small group of jackdaws were busily scrounging pellets from the feed hoppers of a shoot. The shoot manager felt these camp followers were best removed before eggs became an option on the menu, so using standard wire netting covered sections as walls, his keeper built a crow trap next to the laying pen. In its first month this trap caught forty jackdaws, six magpies and half a dozen other assorted corvids. Meanwhile the original small group of jackdaws still seemed to be around the place. Crows are a bit like rats: when you see one, you probably have a dozen.

Ways of controlling egg stealing from laying pens are well documented. The wise shoot manager uses, or authorises use of, whatever legal remedies are necessary.

Flock mating large numbers of pheasants in one pen is undoubtedly cost effective. It is however nice to produce a few pure bred pheasant to mingle with the majority. This can easily be achieved by establishing two or three mini pens adjacent to the main pen. If the best of the caught-up melanistic mutants, bohemian, white or whatever hen birds, plus appropriate cock pheasant are tucked into such mini pens, then you will have a supply of such birds for next season. There is no need to keep the eggs separate; as soon as they hatch, most variants are readily apparent.

Where ducks are to be included in the rearing programme on anything but a nominal scale, there are advantages in having a separate duck laying pen which can be on dry land. It is ideally made by putting a netting fence around a small pond. But do ensure that no fox, mink or otter can come strolling out of that large field drain which empties into one side of the chosen pond.

In small numbers, red-legged partridge can take their chances in the hurly burly of a communal laying pen. If you want to get eggs on a larger scale, then mini pheasant laying pens, made of a few wire netting covered sections, are the answer. Red-legged partridge are delightful people for most of the year. While laying however, hen birds do sometimes develop psychopathic tendencies which manifest themselves in occasional rather gory lynchings of their fellows, by scalping. Once a bird has been attacked, it must be removed from the pen immediately; if this is not done the victim will be dead within hours. Fortunately, this murderous phase passes, and does not usually become a real problem.

Grey partridge are delightful birds, but cannot be flock mated. If you want to produce eggs, they must be put into separate pens, so the whole exercise is equipment and labour intensive. On top of this, wild caught grey partridges are very inclined to go on 'no lay' strikes, rather like political prisoners going on hunger strike. Aviary reared grey partridge are better layers, but that means keeping them penned up all year. Game farmers do this very well, so the eggs you buy from them will usually be far better value than trying to produce your own.

Once a laying pen or pens are organised, the catching-up of stock birds can commence. Methods of catching-up pheasants have changed little over a hundred years. Most old-type catcher's systems still seem quite effective. Some people have a talent for this type of work, others don't. When a shoot manager finds out that his keeper comes into this second category he should, as diplomatically as possible, delegate the work elsewhere. There is usually a retired gamekeeper or reformed, one-time poacher, around who can be trusted.

People tend to be lax about checking and emptying their pheasant catchers. The thinking seems to be that, once the pheasant is caught, he won't get out, so why the rush? The reason for the rush is that pheasants in catchers are very vulnerable. Foxes, badgers, stray dogs and other predators are a real menace. They may not be able to break into the catchers and kill the bird – sometimes they can – but such attacks cause trapped birds vast distress and often physical injury. A pheasant which has virtually battered itself to death may not, at the outset, show external signs of damage. Nor does the freshly dropped apple, but within a day or so, the damage is apparent in both cases. Accordingly, all pheasant catchers should be checked as early as possible in the morning, as late as possible in the evening, and once around midday. The hungry early morning pheasant, fresh out of its roost tree, is especially attracted to a wheat baited trap. This is just the time when the hungry fox is going home after an unsuccessful night's hunting.

Red-legged partridge – or those hybrids which we now call red-legs – often facilitate their being caught. Like hares, they are attracted to broadleaf woodland, and often end up there when the weather gets severe. If red-legs are in the vicinity, it is not unusual to catch a whole covey, at one fell swoop, in a woodland pheasant catcher.

Small numbers of wild ducks for the laying pens can be caught via standard pheasant catchers located on lakeside or riverbank. Where larger numbers of duck are required, the most effective way of ensnaring them is via a wet-and-dry duck trap. This is an aviary-like contraption, which ideally becomes a fixture at the desired catching point. Half the catcher extends out over the water, the rest encloses dry land. There is a human access door in the dry end. Two falling gates or doors are the main moving parts. One closes the wet or water end, and extends below the surface. The other shuts off the dry end. When not in use, wet-and-dry gates are wired open. The catcher becomes a main duck feeding point and shooting in that vicinity is avoided.

Mallard duck start laying in March, so prospective stock birds need to be caught-up as soon as possible after Christmas. Prior to the start of catching, all feeding should be concentrated in and around the wet end of the duck catcher. The catcher is made ready, enabling both gates to be released by a string or wire which leads to a suitable hiding place.

Duck always feel safer on water than on land. A majority of birds which come to feed will stay afloat, up-ending for whatever grain or feed is around. When the wet gate is activated it falls with a splash. Duck caught inside fly up to the dry end, then whizz around in a general panic. The human trapper must now get the ducks into the dry end as quickly as possible or they will escape by diving under the wire netting sides. He does this by leaping into the water at the wet end, and dropping the dry gate as the birds surge away from him.

There follows an exciting, muddy and smelly time, catching, brailing and crating up the mallard for removal to the laying pen. At the end of this exercise, most active participants are noticeably in need of a bath and change of clothes!

A word of caution: to be effective, duck catchers tend to be located in quiet, out of the way places. It is not unknown for poachers to use these catchers at night, for purposes other than that for which they were built. To avoid this, the two falling gates should be wired very firmly open, better still, dismounted and stored away from the trap.

When catching mallard, surplus drakes should *not* be released until the whole catching programme is completed. Put them back on the lake too soon and for weeks they won't go within a mile of the dreaded wet-and-dry catcher. Word seems to spread to other ducks, and catch success declines steeply.

When catching pheasants for laying pens there is a widespread practice amongst gamekeepers to knock on the head all surplus cock pheasants. On a larger shoot this amounts to some hundreds of pheasants. Game dealers are happy to take them and the cash proceeds tend to go into the keepers' pockets. This is seen as a perk of the job, but perk or not, it is a scandalous waste of good birds. Any shoot manager who claims to run a cost-effective shoot should ban the practice, which seems to be based on two old gamekeeper arguments, both of which are seriously flawed.

The first argument suggests that spare cock pheasants interfere with hen birds; as a result nests get deserted or fail. This argument conveniently ignores the *raison d'être* of catching-up pheasants for egg production. Like it or not, the year-on-year breeding success of wild pheasants in Britain is mediocre. Whether there is one cock pheasant in the immediate vicinity or a dozen, most hen pheasants will make a nonsense of nesting. Attacks by crows, foxes and badgers and disturbance by cattle, dogs, humans and agricultural processes, all contribute to hatching failures. The minority of broods which do hatch stand a real chance of being decimated by bad weather.

Later in the season when the weather is less inclement, ground cover more dense, and predators less hungry, wild pheasants often do produce small broods. These are the squeakers seen in harvest fields and few of these late season birds survive to become viable adults.

A second argument for slaying cock pheasants in the spring is that they encourage young poults to wander. All who have studied pheasants closely over the years know this to be another fallacy; all pheasants roam and adult birds do so to a routine pattern. That is why a particular wood or sandpit has to be shot at a particular time of day. Outside of that period, the place may be void of birds.

Before she gets involved with breeding, a hen pheasant may wander a mile down the valley each morning and half a mile up the hill that afternoon. When her brood are still of tender age, they get taken on these daily route marches. Those which don't die en route quickly get to know the district, and how to find the way home. They also learn how to roost up in trees rather than squatting on the ground at night. In the absence of pheasant mothers to show them how its done, a levening of old cock birds in the woods establishes the 'follow my leader' principle. This helps stabilize the mindless platoons of young poults, which otherwise march over the hills and far away.

A third good reason for keeping old cock birds is this: come those early November shoots, these will be the real high fliers.

To get best value from the cost and effort expended on egg production, the shoot manager should do all he can to generate a good supply of *early* eggs. With bees and honey producing potential in mind, the old saying suggested:

A swarm in May is worth a load of hay
A swarm in June is worth a silver spoon
A swarm in July is not worth a fly

The situation with game bird eggs is not totally dissimilar; time is very much of the essence. As a rule of thumb: one pheasant egg in mid-April is worth two in mid-May, or four in mid-June. *You* may not need early eggs for your particular shoot programme, others will.

The majority of wild pheasants in Britain hatch during the first two weeks of June. The bulk of these birds will not have long tails, or be properly muscled-up and flying well, until the second part of November, six weeks or so after the season opens. Many shoots accept this as a fact of life and don't plan main days pheasant shooting until late November. However commercial shoots, and some larger syndicate shoots, are often under pressure to start pheasant shooting, with acceptable birds, just as soon as possible in October. This is where those early eggs have a role to play.

A wild hen pheasant probably takes three weeks to lay her full clutch of eggs. Local weather conditions during early spring influence the start date, but this is usually mid to late April. By comparison, the sister of that wild hen bird, put in a laying pen in January and leading a well fed and uneventful life thereafter, will typically come into lay a week or two earlier. These early pheasant eggs, if incubated straight away, produce day-old chicks in early to mid May, which is a full month ahead of their wild cousins. The same applies to the bulk of shoot/game farm reared birds.

Now a month may not seem long to a human. To a game bird however, spending the first weeks of life at a time when hours of daylight are still stretching out, day by day, is a huge advantage. In any passable summer, these May hatched pheasants from early eggs will have long tails and be flying like adults by mid October.

Another group of people with great interest in early eggs are those who want double usage out of expensive game rearing equipment. The problem here tends to be, how quickly can the first batch of birds be weaned off heat, in order to free the brooders for newcomers? This is usually about four weeks. The sooner the first batch gets started, the earlier the 'second team' birds can be started.

The shoot which can produce early eggs and has no use for them, or is prepared to part with them, can, with ingenuity, trade them with neighbouring shoots or game farmers. Eggs, day-olds and even poults at some later stage, can be arranged on distinctly favourable terms. At the other end of the egg production scale, those laid after mid June tend to become as valuable as a bee swarm in July. Late chicks can be a drug on the market and are often very cheap. The last thing most shoot managers want is crowds of short tailed, immature birds struggling past guns in late November. However, if you happen to have an isolated wood, quarry, pithole or whatever, which holds birds well, and from which they are unlikely to leach into the main coverts, a batch of these late, low cost birds can be worth buying. By Christmas time they may be reasonable pheasants.

To get stock birds laying early, you really need to catch them up early. Pheasant, ducks and red-legged partridges should all be caught as soon as possible after Christmas. This has three advantages: these birds don't get shot or wounded during the last weeks of the season; they are well fed and less stressed, if the weather turns severe during late January or February; they have two to three months before laying commences. An early start to laying also means that you can return stock birds to the woods that much earlier. If the birds are out again by mid May, there is every chance that they will attempt a small clutch of eggs in the wild. As is the way with pheasants, many of these wild nests will fail, but some will succeed. The vegetation and herbage is better grown by that time, nests are slightly less vulnerable to predators, so chicks which hatch have improved survival prospects. Those which make the grade will be well grown by late November, and a nice bonus for the shoot.

So far there has been a marked bias in this chapter towards the production of game bird eggs via laying pens. It would be wrong however to totally ignore wild eggs. Despite attempting to catch up as many hen birds as possible, you will never get the lot. Some hen pheasants seem prepared to starve if needs be, rather than follow that appetizing trail of wheat into the catcher. Maybe they are naturally bright; more likely, they remember what happened to them last year! Either way, there will be a number of birds who nest or attempt to nest around the shoot.

Certainly up to the middle of May, all possible eggs should be picked up. With practice it is not desperately hard to find pheasant nests and if you have a dog with some talent, it will often find them for you. The author had a golden retriever who was mustard at finding nests. He moved so fast that, especially in mowing grass or winter cereals, he regularly grabbed the hen bird off her nest, which was not the intention or desirable. In the ensuing scuffle, eggs would scatter like snooker balls, and some got broken. It just goes to show, however, if a gun dog can track a pheasant to its nest and grab it, so too can any fox worth its salt.

Some of these eggs picked up around the shoot are bound to be 'hot' or part incubated. In this condition they do not survive being cooled down and stored, before being sent with a batch to the main incubator. For this reason, every shoot should have at least one still air incubator. This needs to have a reasonable capacity, (say) one hundred and fifty or more pheasant eggs. It is switched on in early April and stays running until the egg season is over. Eggs for this type of local incubator can come from unlikely sources. A bantam hen and a guinea fowl shared a nest in some nettles behind the author's log shed. These eggs were collected fairly regularly but always leaving one old hen egg to keep the nest 'alive' and stop the joint owners laying elsewhere. In due course a hen pheasant started to lay in the same nest. Now, pheasant can attract adverse publicity to themselves by laying random eggs amongst those of partridge, and causing the rightful nest owner to desert. From this experience it seems that pheasants themselves are not in the slightest bit perturbed at consistently laying eggs amongst those of other species. A mixture of white bantam eggs, speckled guinea fowl eggs and olive green pheasant eggs, hardly looks like a typical clutch for any bird. Whether or not the respective owners of this 'time share' nest ever met each other is not known, but the hen pheasant alone laid over twenty eggs. As a result there were probably ten more pheasants around the shoot that autumn.

As assorted eggs get found, rescued, salvaged or whatever, load them into the local incubator. If the humidity is kept well up, such incubators can become like assembly lines. Eggs go in the top and chicks are collected from the bottom. Just two points to remember here: firstly, write a date on each egg when it goes in and every week ensure those which are well overdue, and therefore duds, are thrown out. If you don't do this, smelly explosions can take place. Secondly, *under no circumstances* mix duck eggs, or goose eggs with those of other fowl. If you do, there is every chance of getting salmonella permanently in the incubator. This will have no effect on ducklings or goslings, but it can decimate newly hatched pheasants, partridge, domestic fowl, guinea fowl and the like, forever after. Eggs of this latter group can, incidentally, be jumbled up together in an incubator with no obvious harm. Guinea fowl eggs however, have a depressingly low hatch rate in most incubators. Later in the book we suggest that a few guinea fowl be turned out into the pheasant coverts. In all respects other than hatching, guinea fowl can be mixed with, and treated like, pheasants. But if you want to get day old chicks in the first instance, put your guinea fowl eggs under a chicken. If ducks are a feature of the shoot, and you produce your own eggs, it is essential to have one or more separate incubators marked 'ducks'. Only the eggs of web footed species go into this machine.

With reasonable care, a still air incubator lasts for many years and it can pay for itself in the first season. The same cannot be said for high capacity force draught commercial incubators. Those who flinch from capital expenditure on shoot related matters, must seriously brace themselves before contemplating purchase of a commercial incubator.

The real problem for a shoot, or indeed a game farmer, is the fact that the game bird egg hatching season only lasts about eight weeks. The commercial poultry or turkey breeder can think in terms of using his incubator for a dozen or more hatching cycles each year. By comparison the game farmer is lucky to get three hatches a year, most shoots get less than two, so, how many years does it take for a big shoot incubator pay for itself?

Earlier generations of commercial incubators were very dependent on operator skills and also mechanically unreliable. Few people who have dealt with such machines cannot recount horror stories where thousands of eggs get written off due to machine faults, operator blunders or power failure. What happened to all those old incubators? A not insignificant number eventually found their way into sheds and outbuildings behind keeper's cottages. There they can be found to this day.

It takes a lot of time, effort and cash for a shoot to produce some thousands of game bird eggs. Furthermore, if that lot get lost or destroyed, they cannot easily be replaced. Stock birds cannot suddenly be called upon to lay another thirty eggs each and even if they could, time has been lost. This means later birds, less well grown and, if not inferior, certainly later sport that year. To put all those literal eggs into one metaphorical incubator basket, is tantmount to playing Russian roulette. You may survive, but is it worth the risk?

Throughout this book there is a noticeable and recurring theme: make full use of existing talent, resources and facilities on the shoot. Egg incubation is one big area where *risks should not be taken*. If a shoot incubator is of modern design, fully automatic and new or virtually new – fine. If not, ignore the tears and tantrums of an old keeper, who loves that incubator like a brother; harden your heart and opt for contract hatching. There is no dramatic shortage of pheasant egg hatching capacity in most parts of Britain. Talk with shoot neighbours and/or local game farmers. Negotiate a contract hatching deal; it may well be possible to pay the whole cost with spare eggs, or with day-old chicks that are surplus to shoot needs.

4 : *Rearing and Release*

A shoot manager may or may not chose to produce eggs, to rear birds, or indeed to release anything on his land. Some shoots are blessed with ideal conditions for attracting, holding, and showing wild birds. A few big shoots and many small ones, never rear or release anything. With a programme of predator and poacher control and some judicious feeding, they do surprisingly well.

It is not unknown for those with proprietorial or shooting interests in successful wild bird shoots, to be mildly scathing about other types of shooting. In terms of visible sporting qualities of birds presented, there are elements of truth in what they say. Some such individuals, however, are skating on thin ice. It is not unknown for reputed wild bird shoots to be brought to their knees when large estates some miles away suddenly stop rearing birds! Obviously, given highly favourable terrain, even so-called mediocre birds can look impressive. Unless favoured by the gods with ideal land and local climate, or unless a very modest programme of shooting is planned, most shoot managers will need to turn out some birds. Whether they rear these birds at home or buy them in as grown poults, is a local decision. Time and cost are obvious criteria.

Ascertaining the cost of bought in poults does not involve cerebral gymnastics or a degree in mathematics. The price list of a local game farmer tells all, but costing a do-it-yourself operation is more complex.

Operational expenses such as labour, electricity, gas, feed, medications, wing tags, brailes, and temporary rent of buildings, are all fairly straightforward. Capital costs, for wire netting, pens, supply of power and water to new locations, equipment such as incubators, brooders' hoppers and drinkers, are not in themselves difficult to add up. Most shoot managers, however, will need accountancy advice regarding how such costs are best charged, over which period of time and against what.

Marginal costs of becoming embroiled with game bird rearing are difficult enough to ascertain, even with hindsight. Forecasting is especially tough. These costs typically cover enhanced telephone and petrol bills, loss of wife's car (written off by gamekeeper on shoot errand), cost of placating wife for this, and other occasions when shoot activities impinge adversely on family life, and so on.

At the end of the day, a well run shoot which has to pay commercial rates for all labour, consumables and service, is likely to produce pheasant poults for much the same *cost* as a game farmer. The shoot therefore saves itself the mark-up or profit which keeps the game farmer in business. On a thousand poults, this will be a not insignificant sum. But most shoot managers can do better than that. With determination, wit, charm and ingenuity, other cost savings can be made. Volunteer or part-time labour can replace paid professionals. Low cost or subsidised power is sometimes available. Less expensive feed stuffs, and use of local facilities, can also make useful contributions. The Game Conservancy regularly publish comparative figures of shoot costs which, year after year, highlight the points just made. In cost control terms, some shoots perform notably better than others. Costs and revenue are discussed more fully in Chapter 10.

It is not the purpose of this chapter to provide a detailed treatise on all aspects of gamebird rearing. For instance: if and when to debeak, and how to do it. We suspect that relatively few shoot managers get involved with personally debeaking two thousand poults in any one day. If they do, they will very soon know every bit as much about the subject as does the author. We also suspect that, next year, they will chose to delegate this particular character building activity to someone else! The main purpose of this chapter is to comment on how gamebird rearing and release on both large and smaller scales, can be achieved with a minimum waste of money, time and birds.

Main operational costs which confront the would be rearer of gamebirds are threefold: power, feed and labour. On the face of it, cost cutting in any of these areas is fraught with risk. Turn down the heaters and chicks die or fail to grow properly; give inadequate or inappropriate feed and the same thing happens. Skimp on labour or supervision and all sorts of problems can occur, for instance feather picking, and even more seriously, vent pecking and cannibalism. If not stamped on very quickly, such vices can spring up almost overnight and sweep away hundreds of young pheasants. Sickness and disease are also ever present threats. As with psychopathic tendencies, they can take hold like a bushfire, and wreak fearful damage. Close supervision of young birds is the only way to keep on top of the situation.

One obvious way to improve rearing efficiency is to house the whole operation in a decent building or range of buildings. Far too many gamekeepers are wedded to a motley assortment of sheds, caravans, plywood contraptions and pens. This shanty town is collected together annually in a field, somewhere behind his house, and given the grand name 'rearing field'. Especially with regard to heating costs and labour, most such operations are desperately inefficient. In addition, no matter how much scrubbing and creosoting goes on, wooden structures used year after year for rearing become a real health risk for young birds. Lice, mites, parasites and disease all tend to become endemic in the structures.

By comparison heater banks and pens, assembled in a secure weatherproof and vermin proof building, have a lot to offer. A great cry of protest is the usual keeper reaction to any suggestion that his shanty town be replaced by a more modern rearing system. Move the operation to farm buildings up the road, and everything which does not get stolen will die – goes the cry. It is human nature to react against

(*above*) Cock pheasant: this is my territory.

PLATE 1

(*left*) Where possible, feed hoppers should be painted the same colour – regardless of shape and size.

PLATE 2

(*above*) A catcher for laying pen birds.
(*below*) Midday, and the score mounts: eggs from wild pheasant nests.

(*above*) See me go – a hare shows his paces.

PLATE 3

(*left*) A fine buck: roe stalking can provide extra revenue for the shoot.

PLATE 4

The roebuck stalker.

PLATE 5

(*above*) Pheasant on a frosty morning, and (*below*) A partridge to hand.

PLATE 6

(*above*) Feeding the flight pond, and (*below*) Duck shooting – a simple but effective hide.

PLATE 7

(*above*) Duck arrive, and (*below*) Mallard drake to hand.

PLATE 8

(*above*) Beaters – fine men, slow transport.
(*below*) Beaters in tall kale, thankful it's a dry day.

change, so this response is not surprising. At the end of the day, persistent adverse reaction may be more a product of local keeper/farmer relationships, than of doubt regarding technical merit and advantages which could accrue.

Buildings suitable for game rearing operations need not be large, modern or impressive; they can be small, old and unimpressive, and still work very well. They must of course be weatherproof and secure against unauthorised intrusions; windows and other light sources must be capable of shading, without too much work, and a level concrete floor is a great advantage. The shoot only needs to use such buildings for two or three months between May and July. They are more readily available on a short let basis than is widely assumed. The farming industry has become very progressive where building utilisation is concerned. The time was when a potato store was a potato store, and used for little else, so it stayed empty for three quarters of the year. The aim now is to make buildings work all the year round. So, the grain store of autumn becomes the cattle yard of winter and perhaps the lambing shed of spring. By the time a shoot comes looking for building space, a fair bit will be standing empty. Old season crops have gone and new ones not arrived, bagged fertilizer has been spread, livestock is out to grass.

When choosing a building, the shoot manager must do some detective work regarding prior occupancy. The one thing to be avoided at all costs is a building which has been used by any domestic poultry at any time in the past. It is also highly advisable not to be even near a farmyard complex which houses any form of intensively reared poultry. In most cases these provisos do not seriously limit choice.

When shoot usage is over, farm building rented for a couple of months or so will usually have to be cleaned. Bird droppings baked onto concrete by heaters can be extremely difficult to remove. A small investment in rolls of strong brown paper at the outset can be well worthwhile. This is used to cover the concrete floor within all areas where circular hardboard pens around heaters, or wire netting section pens are assembled. At the end of the day, the paper can be lifted, and cleaning is greatly simplified. The word 'strong' should perhaps be emphasised regarding paper for the floor. If it is too thin, the paper sticks to the concrete, especially where drinkers have been standing. Newspaper is dreadful in this respect; it also gets shredded by bored pheasant poults, and probably creates more mess than it is worth.

When ducklings are reared, they should ideally be in a separate building from that which houses pheasants, partridge or guinea fowl. Failing that, physical separation in some way is essential to ensure that never the twain meet. Reasons for this separation are exactly those which relate to keeping separate incubators for duck eggs: ducks and ducklings can be carriers of diseases, which are very bad news indeed for non webbed foot species.

Young ducks are not difficult to rear. They are essentially genial and gregarious and lack that inclination to commit grevious bodily harm to their fellow which seems to lurk in the breast of all young pheasants. One negative thing: ducklings do produce copious quantities of very watery droppings. Some highly absorbent forms of litter such as peat or sawdust is essential to keep them clean, dry and free from the cement-like droppings which get baked onto their down by the heaters.

Another point about rearing ducklings: with pheasants, there is rarely a problem of birds getting too tame, any tendency in this direction soon disappearing when pheasant poults are turned out to covert. Young ducks however can get very tame, and stay that way. The problem seems to arise very early in life; it stems from imprinting. Normally this relates to a mother duck but if ducklings get handled too much or even see too much of humans during that crucial first week or so of life, they can get adversely imprinted. Once this happens, it does not readily wear off, even when those birds go out to marsh or lake. Imprinting can happen in the most innocent ways; a keeper's small daughter playing with the ducklings while daddy checks the pheasants may be all that is needed. So be careful.

Before a shoot manager takes over part-time use of a building for his rearing operation he must ensure it is adequately insured. Conflagration is not a regular occurrence amongst farm buildings, but straw or hay barns do sometimes go up in flames. There may be confusion as to where the fire started. Some shoot managers insure against loss of birds in the rearing system due to natural disaster, but this can be overly expensive.

An ability to control the level of lighting is important where birds are reared intensively. Too much light and young pheasants can become hyperactive and hyperaggressive. Too little light and they don't eat and don't grow. Making a building thoroughly predator proof can be harder than it seems. This factor alone may be dominant when deciding upon which particular buildings to use. Cats can be especially troublesome and their powers of athleticism must not be under-rated.

As an emergency measure, a stable was being prepared for a hundred or so unexpected day-old pheasants. The place had been mucked out, swept and was almost ready when a strange scrabbling noise was heard. A stable cat could vaguely be seen peering from a cobweb covered gap between the stable wall and roof. When it saw that all the bumping and cleaning noises were being made by friendly people which he knew, the cat promptly squeezed through an impossibly small gap and jumped down inside to be congratulated. If a well fed but mildly curious cat can get through such a small gap, think what a really hungry cat can do when the building is full of chicks.

Game bird chicks get lost to some unusual predators. An old bantam hen had been given an assorted bunch of homeless young pheasants to foster. For safe-keeping they were shut in a calf box. This bantam had the fighting properties of Queen Boadicea: no dog or cat ever dared approach when she had chicks. As a result she very rarely lost anything but now she did. Within a week, six chicks had vanished into thin air. Now that particular calf box had always been deemed predator proof but there was a small crack in the back wall, at ground level. It seemed too narrow for a rat, so perhaps a weasel was coming in. On hands and knees with a torch, looking for tell-tale ginger hairs, the shoot manager found himself looking at reptile scales. Immediately behind the calf box was a steaming dung heap. An excavation to see what lay on the far side of the crack in the wall revealed a dozen or so membrane covered grass snake eggs. The owner of those eggs was clearly the culprit. A mouse hole led to the cracked wall, so the snake had no difficulty gaining access to the bantam and her brood. Having snatched and swallowed a chick it obviously had difficulty getting out again, with a large bulge in its middle. Maybe the old hen fought a rearguard action. Either way the snake lost scales while escaping. One suspects that not too many game bird chicks get taken in this way. The cat and the snake story serve only to highlight the need for vigilance regarding predator exclusion.

Apart from improved management efficiency, and a need for less gas or electricity to maintain a good ambient temperature, and often less waste of feed, rearing game birds in buildings is conducive to batch rearing. This can also improve cost effectiveness.

Vagaries of egg laying and the variability of hatching success are not in themselves conducive to rearing young birds in neat batches of equal numbers. However, when a shoot rearing programme can cope with (say) 500 young birds at a time, it is very beneficial to have just that number. If 373 day-olds emerge on one occasion and 720 on another, rearing resources are alternately underutilized then overloaded. What can be done? The best plan is to have a mutually beneficial arrangement with a local game farmer or some other contract hatcher of game bird eggs. If this person is already scheduled to contract hatch your eggs, it all becomes that much easier.

At the outset it was suggested that shoot managers should aim to produce eggs in excess of their obvious needs. Here is one of the reasons why. Your shoot may be able to supply a contract hatcher or game farmer with eggs that will result in (say) 4,000 day-old pheasants. If only 3,000 of these are needed for the shoot stocking programme, there is a bargaining surplus of 1,000 day-olds. Given the situation alluded to earlier, a deal can often be organized on the following basis. Regardless of whether 373 or 720 chicks hatch out from eggs which the shoot put in for hatching during a particular week, an exact 500 day-olds is made available; if hatching numbers are down the contract hatcher makes them up from his own stock. If they are up, he absorbs that surplus. Everyone keeps a careful note of numbers. After three weeks, the rearing shoot has 1,500 young birds on the ground; at this point a break period of a week or two may be necessary before a second wave of day-olds can reuse the same brooder/heater/pen facilities. During break periods, the hatcher may absorb all surplus birds. Alternatively, the rearing shoot may collect them to supply a neighbour or to sell them elsewhere. Subsequently day-olds at 500 per week are made available for another three weeks.

At the end of the hatching season there is settling up on a previously agreed basis. The contract hatcher claims hatching costs of eggs delivered to him, and costs of making up numbers to an agreed chick batch size, at so much per bird. Against all this, the rearing shoot offsets cost of surplus birds retained by the contract hatcher. With any luck the shoot has a positive balance. Alternatively no money changes hands and both sides are happy.

When new rearing programmes are first introduced, an element of fine tuning is usually necessary. A batch size of 500 day-olds may seem fine in theory but after a couple of weeks, as birds begin to grow rapidly, overcrowding may occur. It may be possible for pens, or enclosures to be enlarged or alternatively the batch size may be scaled down, and future numbers reduced to say 400 day-old chicks at a time. Once the right balance is achieved, the whole rearing programme can become markedly more stress free for birds and humans alike. The cost per bird reared also tends to become more acceptable.

Regardless of how sophisticated a rearing programme becomes in terms of egg production, hatching, and use of buildings for batch rearing – broody hens should not be ignored. With very little fuss, cost or effort, a few old hens can put a hundred or so birds into your woods each year that would otherwise be lost.

Broody hens, like heavyweight hunters, should be judged by performance and not by looks. The skills of our grandfathers when it came to making poultry work have to some extent been lost. They thought nothing of making a good sitting hen hatch two or more batches of eggs, one after the other. Once a hen got into the rearing phase, there was no need to be limited to one batch of chicks. With careful introducing, the right sort of broody hen was and is, willing to become a feathered Dr Barnardo, and foster whatever comes along. The operation has to be handled with some sensitivity, especially with novice broodies. Introduction of new chicks in the early evening seems the safest time, if rejection prospects are to be minimised. The best the author has managed was one old hen with a mixture of pheasant, guinea fowl and domestic fowl chicks. They all ate the same food, and lived happily together for several weeks as one large multi-racial family. A few orphan mallard so reared in the author's yard chose to remain domesticated. But even that had led to an expected beneficial result: next spring two of the mallard ducks laid full clutches of eggs in a stable and hatched the lot themselves. These offspring subsequently took that big step into the wild which their parents had not.

Chick casualties are a necesary by-product of all rearing operations, so the objective must be to keep fatalities as low as possible. Some chicks get chilled, others fail to start eating properly or get pecked or trampled, others turn up in incubators at unexpected times. Many shoots have no means of coping with those late hatchers or minor invalids and they get left to take their chances; most die. Quite a few of these chicks can however become viable pheasants, given a less spartan approach. There is no benefit in taking a semi comatose chick which somehow escaped from a pen and got chilled, and putting it back under a heater or lamp with dozens of healthy chicks all scrummaging around – the invalid merely gets flattened. There is a real benefit from putting these and other spare chicks under a broody hen. It cannot but cheer even the hardest of hearts to find in the morning that at least half the near corpses put under a broody last night have revived. Once chicks are fit and well and there is a suitable place for them elsewhere, they should be taken away from the broody, to make room for more.

A few guinea fowl turned out into the woods, are beneficial to a shoot. So far as rearing is concerned, pheasants and guinea fowl can be integrated from day one. If you want to get a reasonable hatch rate from guinea fowl eggs however, do not put them in an incubator – leastwise not unless you are prepared to see most of them fail, dead-in-shell. By comparison with the abysmal results from most incubators, results achieved by broody hens can be exceptionally good. Even those faded, muddy guinea fowl eggs of indeterminate age, found by someone in a nettle patch, seem to hatch with remarkable regularity.

When the open field system ruled supreme, broody hens, in serried ranks of coops, kept watch over their respective broods. A frantic clucking of mother hens called the more attentive chicks to safety when danger threatened. From morning opening, to nightly closure of coops, someone with a gun stood guard on the rearing field. Despite all this effort and vigilance, the wastage of birds between hatching and release phase was considerable. Those young pheasants or partridge which made the grade and survived were predator wise, weatherproof and tough.

The broody hen now plays a very minor role in mainstream rearing activities. In the scramble to produce enough birds during a desperately short rearing season, a heavy emphasis is placed on early life survival. In their first few weeks of life, many open field reared chicks died through getting lost, chilled or snatched by weasels running the mole tunnels. Modern game bird chicks are cosseted: carefully controlled heat and light, exclusion of predators, high protein food, and preventative medications all work wonders. Prior to release, modern pheasant poults can be good-looking, well-grown and precocious. One cannot expect them to be knowledgeable regarding predators but one can expect them to be weather-proof and tough; all too often they are neither.

In the hand, a well hardened off poult and a soft one do not look all that different. The birds are quite naturally scared, and with adrenalin flowing, they all look sharp. Strolling in the sunshine on a fine day they also look pretty much alike. It is only on a wet and blustery day that the hard and the soft birds look like chalk and cheese. The well hardened off bird has tight feathers and looks confident. The soft poult has loose or fluffed out feathers, and looks decidedly uncheerful. Game farmers and shoots which rear, tackle the problem of harden-ing off poults in different ways. Some use mist sprays over the pens, others take them off heat early, and so on. Such methods probably all work to some extent. But that is just it – to *some* extent. Every year hundreds of thousands of inad-equately hardened off pheasant poults get released into British coverts. It then becomes a lottery whether or not they survive. If the weather is congenial and not too wet, a good number make the grade. If they survive their first two weeks in the woods they will be all right. If the weather turns bad, those newly released semi-hardened poults die like flies.

Keepers involved feel implicated in, if not responsible for, such deaths. Visible evidence is gathered by the sackful and removed. Unless a shoot manager is close to the situation, and able to see it with his own eyes, there is every likelihood that the full scale of disaster will not be admitted.

Remembering what it costs to produce or to buy a ten week old pheasant poult, this sort of weather related gamble is quite crazy. Unfortunately there is no magic formula for getting birds properly hardened off. If he is aware of the problem, however, a shoot manager can be that much more careful with his own birds and/or those he buys in.

When buying birds, it is well worthwhile visiting the vendor's establishment to see for oneself how the birds look. Also to ask how they have been hardened off. If a shoot manager has any weatherproof doubts regarding bought in birds, or indeed his own stock, he should insist on these birds being put in a holding pen for some days before they go out to covert. It is far better to subject such birds to the minor stress of double handling than to toss them into the woods to die.

To further load the odds in his favour, a shoot manager should heed weather forecasts and watch the barometer as time approaches to release birds. When things do not look set fair for at least a few days, give serious consideration to holding up release. Any minor aggravations which may ensue are likely to be rewarded by extra birds around the shoot come September.

Release pens for pheasants are bulky, expensive to build and usually in the wrong places. They were probably ideally located twenty years ago; since then land usage has changed, woods have grown up or been cut down, new roads or houses have been built and pedestrian traffic along footpaths has built up. The bold thing to do is build new pens in what appear to be the right places, but that is easier said than done. Unless the shoot manager actually owns the land or is a tenant farmer, he has to heed carefully the length of time he may have to enjoy the benefits of such labours. All too often the view seems to be that, with only two years of the sporting agreement to run, and with no guarantee of its renewal, it's really not financially viable to spend capital on new release pens. This particular nettle needs to be grasped at the start of a new sporting tenancy/agreement/ licence. At least the shoot manager can then look to amortize the capital cost over a sensible number of years.

When a shoot manager plans to install release pens in woods which have hitherto not held pheasants in numbers, he must ensure that the local estate and tenant farmers are agreeable. It must be remembered that some of these people see the shoot, with its keeper and shooting parties, as a confounded nuisance – a cross which has to be borne but not enjoyed. With some justification, farming interests are often convinced that creation of a new release pen will lead to crops being decimated, and farm tracks churned to muddy oblivion, as shoot vehicles forge to and from the new pens. High diplomacy on the part of the shoot manager is often needed if new release pens are to be sited in the right places, without causing excess local distress.

Whether the shoot manager has five hundred or five thousand poults to release he has to decide how best and where best to put them. One school of thought calls for a maximum capacity release pen in the geographical centre of the shoot, into which goes a majority of birds. This theory assumes that whichever way birds may wander, they still stay around for a while. In terms of pen building costs and supervision of birds on site, this concept has financial advantages. In shooting terms this approach smacks of putting all eggs in one basket. It only requires a stray dog or rogue fox getting into that one pen, and great damage gets done. Human thieves can also steal birds rather easily when they are conveniently concentrated. By comparison, the use of several smaller release pens reduces dangers of one apocalyptic accident, and generally enhances a balanced spread of birds across available land.

Prior to releasing pheasant poults, a shoot manager has his last chance to decide whether or not he wants to ring, tag or in some other way mark his birds. Where a new or revived shoot is concerned, or where new release pens have been constructed, it is usually well worthwhile. This sort of effort is, so to speak, double barrelled: the first shot involves fixing tags or rings; the second shot involves retrieval, counting and the analysis of results. Failure with either aspect invalidates the whole exercise.

The basic rule when setting up a bird marking programme is *keep it simple*. Having seen and tried a number of approaches, the author now strongly favours coloured wing tags. For instance, a simple colour code designates main release areas. No effort is made to ascertain whereabouts on the shoot a particular colour tag is found; the important thing is that it gets recovered somewhere *on* the shoot. The part of this programme that tends to fail is at the end of shoot days. Keepers are not always as vigilant as they might be about checking for tags and retrieving those found. If all birds are tagged on the same wing, it is not desperately difficult to keep up the retrieval process. Even those birds handed out to guests without ever going to the game larder, can be checked and discreetly de-tagged in a few seconds. Every retrieved tag goes into a jam jar or box in the keeper's house. It is illuminating at the end of a season to see how many birds from some pens end up on the shoot, how few from other pens are ever seen again. A shoot manager must learn by these findings and adjust next year's release programme accordingly.

For short term identification there is much to be said for adding a plastic 'flag' to the wing tags of a few poults per pen. If the pen is scheduled for blue metal tags, you find some blue plastic material – typically from a feed or fertilizer bag. A small strip of this coloured plastic, about three or four centimetres long is then crimped into the wing tag of some poults. Likewise if the metal tag for another pen is coloured green, you 'flag' a few poults with green plastic strips. Some of these tags will still be just visible when shooting starts, although most get preened off after a month or so. Their real value lies in that immediate post-release period. As young birds gather on feed rides in (say) blue wood, a month or so after release, it is interesting to see if or when young green wood flagged birds move across to join them. Ducks and partridge can all be wing tagged and flagged in the same way. Wing tags are very discreet and only those who look for them, or who pluck the birds, need be aware of their existence. Leg rings are a highly visible and obstrustive way of marking birds.

Release pens for mallard duck, like the catcher described earlier, are best when of the wet-and-dry type. This means that part of the pen covers the bankside, and part extends out over the lake, pond, river or whatever. A wet-and-dry release pen is an especially good way of conditioning young ducks to scuttling back to water when danger threatens, and getting them into the habit of spending long hours afloat – therefore safe – as opposed to snoozing on the bankside, where they are highly vulnerable.

Young ducks seem to thrive in conditions of mud and slime that would kill young pheasants, and do not seem prone to contracting diseases from exposure to land which has been contaminated by adult ducks. For this reason it is perfectly possible to use the duck catcher, installed by the lake as a means of gathering laying pen volunteers, as a part-time, young bird release pen.

Probably the most cost effective release pens for partridge – both red-legged and grey – is made up of four or six wire netting covered aviary sections. A careful study of local cover crops, and some knowledge of when potatoes, carrots, sugar beet or whatever are going to be harvested, is necessary before a shoot manager can plan his partridge release strategy.

The first big difficulty with young partridges reared *en masse*, is to establish them as man-made coveys. This entails weaning them away from the 'football crowd' masses, in which their early weeks of life have been spent. The next problem is to get these newly created coveys properly hefted on territories or patches of land. Get this wrong and, in double quick time, all these coveys start to merge into one monster pack of partridge. The French traditionally resolve the problem by keeping one or two birds permanently caged at one side of the release pen. These call-birds serve to anchor their foster brothers and sisters, calling them back again if they stray. This approach is considered unsporting and should not be practiced in Britain.

During the first few weeks that pheasant poults spend in the woods, a resident and established stock of wild birds can be a great help. There will of course be a certain number of ex laying pen stock birds around but these may not be especially helpful. Many of them are virtual strangers in the woods they inhabit. On a shoot of any size, stock birds may be released miles away from where they were actually caught. Either by good luck or skill a few seem to get reorientated and return to their old territories; many do not and like young pheasants they become prone to wandering.

Practically the only birds which are stabilized in their ways and fully orientated, are those old cock pheasants, discussed earlier. When the wood fills up with mindless young pheasants, these older birds earn their corn. As old birds move from place to place on their daily peregrinations, some young birds follow. They also follow these old birds back to the home covert at the end of the day, and up into a roosting tree, much as they would have followed a mother pheasant. In this way, a nucleus of poults begin to learn their way around, others follow suit, the knowledge spreads.

Most young pheasants in the release pen will never have seen a chicken. Even so, one or two broody or ex broody hens per pen do seem to help stabilize that unruly mob of poults. Most keepers are not keen on having white leghorn bantams flying over the guns in November; they also don't want to risk losing good broody material but with a little care neither happens. The average domestic fowl is too big to follow pheasant poults out through the fox grids on pen entrances and exits. If one wing is clipped to prevent aerial escape, these old hens can usually be retrieved in a month or so, and brought back to civilisation.

It was suggested earlier that a few guinea fowl released in the woods can benefit a shoot. If this is the plan, they should be turned out at the same time as the pheasants. In an ideal world, one of the broody hens is also foster mother to the guinea fowl. When this occurs, the guinea fowl settle down immediately with no trouble. When turned out as 'unaccompanied minors' however, guinea fowl poults are very prone to marching off and never being seen again.

Once they get established and hefted on a given wood, your handful of guinea fowl become very loath to leave. They make excellent watch dogs and they usually spot predators or intruders long before the average pheasant. Furthermore, pheasants that live with guinea fowl seem to appreciate this because they listen to, and heed, guinea fowl alarm calls. Guinea fowl are remarkably alert at night. It is disturbing for the night prowler to have his shadowy presence advertised by a raucous cackling from the treetops. The patrolling keeper also hears the din and knows something is on the move in his woods.

On shoot days guinea fowl are inclined to fly forward to the last big tree in the wood. They then stop and cackle abuse at guns, beaters et al. Unless wanted for the pot, they should really be left. The shoot will then not need to turn out additional young ones for perhaps two or three years. As a rule guinea fowl in the woods are unlikely to breed successfully. There is little danger of the shoot being overrun by them. Wild breeding success is low because all hen birds in a given group habitually lay their eggs in one communal nest. Two or three hen guinea fowl then try, collectively, to incubate a great heap of eggs. None hatch. If by chance there is but one hen guinea fowl around and no sisters to interfere with the nest, then a few wild chicks will sometimes get reared.

5 : Game Strips and Feeding

By early spring, long before the first pheasant egg is laid, the shoot manager needs to have a clear view of the season's objectives. Actions relating to conservation, rearing and release of game birds are the first building blocks towards construction of those ideals. Between rearing birds in summer, and shooting in late autumn and winter, there is a period of several months. How and where game birds are fed during these lazy days of summer and autumn, and also the extent to which natural cover, game strips and commercial crops provide a congenial environment, has a big influence on subsequent shooting success. Game strips and feeding are therefore the next building blocks to put in place.

Pheasants do not respond well to hardship. They like to be comfortable, well-fed and unmolested. When these conditions do not prevail the relatively few older birds on the ground who are firmly hefted on territories may put up with it. Young birds which comprise the vast bulk of pheasants on the shoot each autumn, do not: they move to pastures new. At worst they wander clear off the place; at other times they gravitate to an especially favoured part of the shoot. The shoot manager then finds that, instead of having two hundred or so birds in each of five woods, he has a thousand birds in one wood and nothing to speak of in the others. This does not help the shooting programme.

Before he can make any decision regarding the number and the siting of game strips, the shoot manager needs to know what agricultural and forestry activity is planned. Most farmers know months ahead what they expect to be doing; foresters plan years ahead. There may be no logic in releasing a hundred or so young partridges onto the old race course this summer as the place is going to be torn about by land drainage in September. Middle hill wood may be due for thinning this winter so unless that can be delayed until after Christmas, it may be wise to give that particular release pen a holiday for the year, and forget about the two good drives it can provide. The only way a shoot manager can find out about such moves is by talking with those who farm and those who manage woodlands on the shoot. This liaison should be ongoing, not just in the shooting season or when there is a crisis. Good relationships between all those who share the land are very important.

As crops rotate, and as economic factors encourage one branch of agriculture and stress another, the vegetation cover across a shoot can vary widely from year to year. Sometimes this is beneficial to game conservation, other times not. In a good year, small blocks of potatoes, turnips, kale, carrots and other 'game friendly' crops, are well distributed across the shoot. In a bad year, great blocks of less desirable cover crops, like sugar beet, may engulf one end of the shoot. Roots and other attractive crops may fringe perimeter fields. When oceans of one cover crop engulf woodland coverts, it can be very hard to hold birds in those woods, until the crop is lifted.

For the most part the shoot manager is not in a position to alter what crops get planted where, or when. He can however, given goodwill within the farming community, influence harvesting or crop lifting arrangements. The time comes to strip graze that chest high kale which butts onto the shoots main block of woodland. It may not make a great difference to the farmer involved how that kale gets cleared. If he can be persuaded to open a strip alongside the wood, and then graze his beasts out towards the open field, an increasing swathe of open land soon appears. Until such time as the kale dwindles to oblivion, an interesting opportunistic drive can be added to the shoot programme.

Being well-organized and systematic, most farmers have a series of maps indicating all their fields, coloured to show what crops are to be planted where; indicative harvest dates are often added. The sooner this information gets transferred onto the shoot manager's master map of the place, the better able he will be to make meaningful decisions regarding release pens, game strips, feed points and so on. Once he knows what the crop pattern will look like for the coming year the shoot manager can get to grips with game strip needs. Some years he may see the need for very few; other years more will be necessary to counter any imbalance, or general lack of agricultural cover crops. When tackling a new shoot, or if a shoot manager is new to the job, he is well advised to discuss the positioning of strips with local farmers. They will often have valuable advice regarding past triumphs and disasters, when certain shooting measures were tried.

Some shoots have an agreed acreage of game cover strips which will be available each year. For this, a seasonal charge per acre is either included in the annual rent, or billed separately. There is also the question of paying for the seed, fertilizer and cultivation processes necessary to get these strips established.

Land wanted for game strips often extends along headlands or beside tracks and farmers can see advantages in not attempting to grow commercial crops in such places. Land compaction by turning vehicles, also shading from trees or hedges is often a problem. Damage by rabbits, and of course game birds, all help to make such places notoriously less productive than more favoured parts of the same field. It can make sense to get paid an acreage rent by the shoot for loss of commercial use, rather than have such land growing scraggy commercial crops.

Game strips need to be planted as early in spring as possible. In many cases they will be alongside cereal crops or pasture. Their job is not only to provide cover and shelter in the shooting season, but also in late summer and autumn.

When cereals have been harvested and autumn cultivation gets under way, a lot of shooting land suddenly becomes bare and exposed. Unless very lucky with the weather, many of those mixtures of seeds, broadcast and rotavated some time in late May or June, will produce plants on the game strip that are still 'knee high to a bee' in September. Birds which have moved out of the wheat and barley, find no shelter there when ploughs and harrows clank around the fields so they move elsewhere. No matter how well a game strip recovers and grows-on in an Indian summer, much of its real benefit will have been lost; birds have to be coaxed back.

Farmers may be ready to provide some game strips, but often have firm views on where they *don't* want them. Who pays how much for what, also needs to be determined. When discussing such matters with farmers, there are five cards which strengthen the shoot manager's hand.

The haggle card	All farmers like to haggle
The shoot card	Most farmers like to shoot
The farmer card	Most farmers don't like other farmers
The cash card	All farmers like cash
The bargain card	All farmers like bargains

The haggle card is self explanatory. All who have spent their formative years in cattle markets or Arab bazaars, know that you never agree to the first price offered. *The shoot card* is subtle. Nothing can be promised: the implication is that cooperative farmers get odd days of free shooting during the season. If he plays the shoot card, the shoot manager must ensure this becomes reality. It rarely involves the shoot in any great sacrifice. Sooner or later in every shoot season, adverse weather, illness, strikes, crashes, family crises, and the like, result in someone not turning up to shoot. Suitably motivated local farmers seem able to extricate themselves from agricultural matters, change into shooting kit, drive five miles and be ready to move off with the guns, all in a staggeringly short space of time.

The farmer card is not subtle. Most farmers are not wildly keen on other farmers, especially the immediate neighbours. They particularly resent other people operating agricultural machinery on their land. The farmer card gives your tenant farmers or whatever, the chance to plant necessary game strips himself, and be paid normal agricultural contractor rates for doing the job. *The cash card* involves offering to pay for work done in folding paper, and not by cheque.

Finally comes *the bargain card*. This again involves little sacrifice to the shoot, and can indeed be a bargain to the farmer. The first step in playing this card is to forget about all those amazing seed cocktails, so beloved by agricultural merchants and game farmers. The type which seems to include everything from sunflowers to maize and lupins to globe artichokes! With every respect to Wisley and Kew gardens, who no doubt specialize in cultivating those luxuriant growths pictured on promotional material, most multi-species mixtures are a dismal failure. Conditions which suit one variety are invariably bad for another. Even sunflowers, which seem to triumph over most adversity and look marvellous in late summer, are rarely worth the space they take. In a typical British climate, field grown sunflowers develop chronic mildew at an early point in time, seeds fail to ripen and end up shunned, even by hungry finches.

The bargain card secret is to offer to plant game strips comprising nothing but thousand head kale, or fodder beet, or some other crop, which can be grazed by farm animals. Pheasants can be very cheerful in a good strip of thousand head kale; beaters and walking guns do not have to dress like deep-sea divers to walk through the stuff. At the end of shooting, the local farmer can graze these game strips with outdoor stocks, or cut and cart them to feed yarded stock. A 'good bite' in late January or February, is not to be sneezed at.

If the shoot manager plays these five cards well, there is no need for tricks. Everyone is happy.

To properly supervise a feeding programme, the shoot manager must be absolutely clear regarding his objectives. He particularly needs to understand the raw material with which he is dealing – predominantly young pheasants. Also the big differences between wild bred and shoot raised birds. As the wild pheasant poults and its shoot-reared cousin stand together on a sunny ride, they look remarkably similar. The shoot bird may be a little bigger, the wild bird may have brighter and tighter feathers – but nothing much else is visible.

The big difference between these birds is inside their heads. At ten or twelve weeks old the wild bird is a positive veteran of the woods and fields. Within a very few days of hatching off, most wild hen pheasants resume daily peregrinations around the district. Struggling and scrambling to keep up, the wild chicks are led down the valley to feed and drink in the lower bog. After that it's off to the oakwood, then up the hillside to dustbath and finally back home to the big laurel patch to roost. A heron takes a chick in the bog and a crow snatches another up the hill; one falls in the stream and drowns; another gets lost in the long grass. It is a spartan regime of route marches, and daily hazards, plus a not very attentive mother pheasant. The handful of young birds still around as poults are not only weather proof and predator wise, but also surprisingly knowledgeable regarding local geography. They can find their way around during the day and back home to those laurels at night. The hen pheasant, and her wild brood often stay together right through to the autumn and beyond, with survivors only finally breaking up in spring. Family togetherness for pheasants is not the same as with partridge, it is more a question of being in the same place at the same time each day, a nodding recognition as birds pass each other, and of roosting in the same massive laurel bush at night.

By comparison with his wild cousin, the shoot reared poult has a mind like a blank sheet of paper, an instruction manual waiting to be written. But his body is active and he is full of energy. Furthermore he is surrounded by dozens of other shoot reared poults, all footloose, feckless and fancy free. Little wonder they are hard to control. Filling the minds of these young birds with just some of that material already absorbed by wild cousins is probably as important as filling their crops with grain.

There are two main parts to the feeding programme. When birds first go out to the woods, the immediate need is to keep them alive. The trauma of being moved, and the dramatic change of surroundings, all takes a little getting over. This means ad-lib feeding in pens, probably with some form of pellets as well as grain, also a quiet stabilizing period. An educational process can then start, first getting birds used to the immediate pen surroundings, then gradually leading them, by trickle feeding, to feed rides and hoppers around the main wood. The aim must be, as early as possible, to condition these birds into viewing the release pen wood in the same light that the wild brood viewed that great laurel bush – as home.

Pheasants, as they mature, become creatures of very fixed habits. Once young poults seem reasonably stabilized in and around the release pen wood, the next job is to impart local knowledge, before they shut their minds to new ideas, or drift away anyhow. The wild birds picked up their information trudging after the hen pheasant. The shoot birds will have to be encouraged and enticed, usually by trickle feeding, plus strategically placed feed hoppers. These hoppers, incidentally, can usually be fabricated by a keeper or local handyman, using chemical spray drums and the like. They do not have to be all the same pattern or size, but they should all be painted the same colour. Before long, young pheasants learn to locate feed hoppers with an intuitive skill, similar to that which enables young children to find ice cream vans.

A word of advice when designing feed hoppers. For the most part these tend to become semi-permanent features around the shoot. In spring they make ideal nesting places for blue tits, field mice and other denizens of the hedgerows. In some ways this does not matter as the young blue tits will have flown by the time the first poults are being released. What does matter is that the hoppers won't work when they have been modified by birds. Nests can be fearfuly hard to remove, so ensure that some cleaning and nest removal flap or lid is incorporated in the hopper design.

One interesting characteristic of pheasants is a disinclination to fly over ground which is unfamiliar. Rather like a steeplechase jockey who views fences before riding over them, pheasants like to walk the course. Soon after birds have been released, the shoot manager needs to review all those drives he has planned for the winter. If he wants to drive birds off that high patch of artichokes and down to the woods below, someone has to start feeding birds up that hill, now. Similarly if birds are to fly across that steep sided valley in November, they must now become familiar with walking down one side, across the bottom, and up the other.

A classic example of birds not being schooled to travel from covert to covert is seen where small woods sit amid big fields. When the wood is driven, all birds break out at one end. They fly around in a huge circle, like planes circling an aircraft carrier at sea, then land back in the wood from which they were disturbed half a minute earlier.

Large scale losses from home reared pheasant poults wandering off can occur on the best run shoots. In addition to running a well-planned feeding programme, a certain amount of dogging-in of straying birds is usually necessary. One particularly hazardous activity for young pheasants is the soon to be outlawed practice of stubble burning. Straw left lying on the ground prior to bailing or burning stubble is a second heaven for young pheasants. Scratching about and burrowing in the straw, it seems to be the occupational therapy which provides most fun.

Farm workers are usually caring people. Even if a gamekeeper is not around to do the job, they typically clear as many poults as possible off the field before it gets lit-up. Where there is ill-will, bad communications or local grudges, this may not happen. The problem is doubly bad where barley fields are involved as the straw burns that much faster and more fiercely. A 'rogue' stubble fire does untold damage in two ways: first it incinerates young birds, which get confused amid the smoke; secondly it so terrifies and disorientates those which survive, that many disappear over the horizon and never come back. The product of months of patient rearing, weeks of careful feeding, and tending, and a lot of shoot cash, can all be lost in minutes. In due course such problems will hopefully be a thing of the past.

An adult pheasant probably doesn't finalize his territory until it is a year old and has bred. After that it becomes very set in its ways. It may have good weather places and bad weather places, morning places and afternoon places, even winter and summer places. At all times however, other than when hen birds are sitting on eggs, it will tend to gravitate at night to one main roosting place.

Migratory birds like some duck and geese which turn up in winter, can have interesting double territories; a nesting territory on some remote Arctic tundra and a wintering territory on a marsh in Britain. It knows both intimately, as well as the thin migratory corridor in between.

The double territories of migratory animals can be most impressive. Apart from deer and foxes which move from hill and moor to valleys when winter strikes, and back again in spring, not all that many British mammals are re-nowned travellers. In Europe, a wild boar may have a summer territory of some thousand acres in a Polish forest. It has a similar sized winter territory in the foothills at the Spanish Pyrenees, and every autumn it treks half way across Europe, from one to the other. Lying-up by day and travelling by night, it follows exactly the same route each year. Through Germany and across France this boar migration has gone on for thousands of years. Every autumn, within a week of the same date, our travelling boar arrives at a small wood in Northern France. It seeks out the pheasant feed hopper, knocks it over and guzzles the spilt grain, sleeps off the meal in a thicket and next night moves on. In spring it returns. Trotting over dark fields, barked at by chained farm dogs, sometimes glimpsed in vehicle headlights by startled motorists, a black and determined looking wraithe. This time the feed hopper stands empty: the boar shows his displeasure by tossing it high into a bush.

On shoots with a population of wild deer, there can be problems with feed hoppers. Deer may not be all that bright, but they soon learn how to extract grain from hoppers, by kicking and butting them. Local countermeasures sometimes have to be considered.

To date we have concentrated very much on the feeding of pheasants. Partridge are much easier to feed because their appetites are much smaller. As with young pheasants, shoot reared young partridge are desperately in need of local education. The normal approach is to try and get them hefted or based on the partridge release pen, and leave them to explore the local surroundings on their own. Sometimes this works, often it does not. The real enemy of the shoot, if it plans to release partridge, is great blocks of sugar beet, kale or similar ground cover crops. No matter how carefully you feed birds, it is usually only a matter of time before they disappear into that ocean of greenery. The chances of getting them back onto the planned release territory is then slight. A great pack of partridge subsequently builds up in the offending crop. When those fields get driven it is impressive for the person who gets one hundred partridges over his head in three seconds but not so impressive for those who get no shooting.

To save costs on the feed bill a shoot manager can do worse than talk to the local miller, or an estate with large scale grain drying equipment. Both categories of people end up with a range of cleanings and screenings which have been removed from the wheat, barley or whatever. Anything which comprises undersized or cracked and shrivelled grains can be used in feed hoppers. It should be noticeably less expensive than good grain but must be clear of chopped bits of straw. If used in hoppers these bits bung up the holes or slots, and are a nuisance. However, grain or near grain with a straw rubbish content is ideal for trickle feeding as bits of straw attract a birds attention to the grain.

Pure chaff with virtually no grain content is another by-product of grain cleaners. The odd sack of this goes down well on a straw covered feed ride – mostly for its occupational therapy use, amusing bored pheasants. The remaining by-products of the grain cleaner will tend to comprise sackfuls of red-shank cleaver and other weed seeds. Unless he keeps canaries, the shoot manager must insist that neither keepers nor shoot helpers bring any such weed seed onto the shoot. If they do, the howls of protest raised by local arable farmers will be heard across the county and such cries are entirely justified. It's not that pheasants don't like such seed, they do. Many such seeds are designed by nature to go straight through pheasants. Furthermore when they emerge into the light of day, the birds intestinal juices have probably cracked any dormancy, thus enabling seeds to germinate straightaway.

When ducks have been released on a shoot or when wild duck are being fed, grain is a simple feed choice – preferably barley. It is also expensive and duck have large appetites and tend to be wasteful eaters. If any large number of birds are involved it is a good idea to find a source of undersized or reject protatoes, or even better, apples. Both these foods seem nicest for ducks when slightly decomposed so they should be tipped into shallow water at the lake side and allowed to 'brew' for a while.

When feeding grain to duck it is interesting to see how quickly the local fish seem to learn about this food bonanza. Coarse fishermen seem to think in terms of boiled grain when choosing bait. When used to the idea, roach will eat hard grain as avidly as goldfish eat ants' eggs.

Once when feeding young ducks, a more than usual level of underwater activity was noticed and it was clear that others were joining the feast. The keeper's small son was dispatched for his fishing rod. With this and a spinner, he hooked three pike in ten minutes, the largest weighing eight pounds. As with the Walrus and the Carpenter's oyster friends, those who go to a feast, sometimes get eaten.

During the months of August and September shoot bills for grain and other feedstuffs can become uncomfortably large. It is well worth while a shoot manager keeping a weekly grain check on how much gets fed in volume terms. At this period in the year, more than at any other time, an accurate view of how many birds are on the place is not difficult to assess. Once shooting is under way, the situation becomes blurred. In early December, when a halfway point in the shoot programme is reached, shoot managers and keepers do not always agree on how many birds are left. Keepers are usually optimistic; shoot managers have to be realistic, since the programme may need to be curtailed

Keeping early season grain records helps to resolve arguments thus: it is known how much feed is now being eaten per week. It is easy to look back and see how much food was being eaten in a typical week in September (when there was also other food around!). It is known how many birds were on the shoot in September, so it cannot be too difficult to estimate present bird numbers. This may seem rough and ready, but it works surprisingly well.

6 : *Shooting Day Preparation*

Summer ends and shooting draws near. To the shoot manager and head keeper it seems a lifetime removed from that chill February day when plans for the new season were first discussed. Much has been done, battles lost and won. What lies ahead?

This is a time when gamekeepers become edgy in the extreme. Any tendencies they may have to stress-related disorders now become apparent. Theirs is an unusual job situation: butchers, bakers and candlestick makers are all judged by the quality and quantity of meat, bread and candlesticks they produce, week after week during the year. By comparison most employers judge their gamekeepers according to what happens on a dozen or so shooting days each winter. Even more interestingly, keepers judge other keepers, and measure their own self esteem, by the same demanding yardstick.

This is probably not a bad thing. It is a good idea, however, for a shoot manager to appreciate keeper sensitivities, as shooting draws near. This is not an appropriate time to suggest a totally new way of tackling traditional drives: the merest hint that the Poplars may be driven in any manner other than the tried and tested, copper bottomed, proven over fifty years method, can cause normally placid gamekeepers to wake screaming in the night. The wise shoot manager keeps interesting ideas such as this under wraps, until later in the season!

Laws decree when the shooting of particular species may start, and when it must stop. Commonsense decrees exactly when a local shooting programme commences. Widely known, even amongst those who never shoot, is the fact that grouse shooting starts on 12 August. This knowledge stems from the remarkable hype and media exposure that the occasion generates. On that particular opening day, restauranteurs and hoteliers vie with each other to be first with grouse on the menu. Newly shot grouse are whisked from heather moor to smart restaurant by motor cycle, helicopter and infinitely more bizarre forms of transport. Goodness knows what grouse taste like after all that!

Less widely known than the opening date of the season is the fact that relatively few grouse meet their Waterloo on that first day. Owners of moors and sporting tenants know that given two or three extra weeks, their grouse will be visibly more mature, and be notably better sporting birds. Later weather is also less likely to be hot and therefore more conducive to grouse driving.

In terms of exactly when to commence shooting, the story with duck, partridge and pheasants, is much the same. All tend to be stronger, and more mature a few weeks into the new season, and most shooting programmes make allowance for this fact.

When reviewing egg production and rearing earlier in this book, brief comments were made on wild duck and partridge. In hard financial terms, neither species can hope to emulate the value-for-money aspect given by pheasants. Duck and partridge tend to cost more to rear, partly because of the necessary small scale of production. End of season recovery rates are usually way below those achieved with pheasants. However, money is not everything. Having a few duck and partridge on the shoot is often a very good idea as they offer the chance to start the lowland season a full month before pheasant shooting begins.

Flight duck in the half-light of a September morning, follow this with a hearty breakfast, then spend the day walking dusty stubbles after partridge. It will not cost too much in cartridges or boot leather, the bag will not be large, but it can be a delightful way to start the shooting season. Throw in a picnic lunch on the sunny side of a straw stack, add congenial company, and such days can become magical, the stuff of which lasting memories are made.

The *quantity* of game shooting over a given block of land is influenced by three main factors: the disposition of natural features, hills, woods, valleys, rivers, reed beds and the like; tactical use of, and success with, specially planted game cover strips; agricultural land usage.

Quality of shooting is much dependent upon the extent and success of rearing and release programmes, and the feeding and management of birds thereafter. The presentation skills of a shoot manager and his gamekeeper are additional factors.

By the start of the shooting season, the shoot manager has effectively dealt himself a hand of cards. They may be better or worse than he expected. His task is now to play those cards to best effect. As a prelude to the first day of shooting, the shoot manager and his keeper, with perhaps a key shoot helper, need to walk all main drives. On this day he must be particularly alert regarding where birds are congregating and how they seem to be moving about the place. For instance, are they walking up that hill to the strip of Jerusalem artichokes mentioned earlier? Evidence may show that a stack of birds are ignoring the blandishments of a trickle line of maize heading uphill, and are daily marching downhill into that neighbouring shoot's potato field. There is still time to modify such habits – but not long.

A gamekeeper lives, eats, breathes and sleeps the shoot upon which he works. As a relative outsider, the shoot manager can see the place with a fresh eye. For this reason he often spots things which are neither obvious nor apparent to the resident man. As they walk the land on the pre-shooting session, the shoot manager must pay attention to crops, herbage and vegetation as well as to birds. Most shoots have areas of dense undergrowth somewhere: at the height of the season, and in adverse weather, these may be parts of key drives, and excellent places for holding birds. In October and November, however, before winter frosts have stripped off leaves and cut down the soft plants, many such woods are effectively impenetrable. At such times they should be left well alone.

On land which has been keepered and shot for many years, all main drives have names. Some of these are obvious: Black Hut drive still has a black wooden forester's hut, Heron Wood had a small heronry in living memory. However, Cage Grove has no trace of cages or aviaries, it is not so called on maps but neither is Fiddlers Hill. Ask any local over the age of sixty, and both features are pointed out with alacrity; local drives take local names. Newly created drives are given names, usually rather unimaginative ones, like upper kale, or lake-side. One new drive became known as Lady Chatterley's!

As he reviews his main drives at the start of the season, a shoot manager notices one important fact: not all drive options will be available all season. Rather like fresh vegetables on the supermarket shelf, most game bird drives have 'best before' dates. Those with the longest 'shelf-life' equivalent, usually relate to natural features. That oakwood on the hillside and the reed bed above the lake, may shoot equally well in January as they do in October. Drives based on carefully planted game strips, however, may have a 'shelf life' closer to weeks than months. By their very nature, such strips are often in exposed places and as the weather gets colder they tend to become less comfortable and less congenial for pheasants. Browsing wild deer and sheep seem to appear from nowhere and start crashing about in such strips, ravenous wood pigeons fall out of the sky. Carefully nurtured strips can be eaten to bare stalks in half an hour – end of game strip, also of farmers hopes of grazing it at the season end.

The shortest 'shelf life' of all, relates to opportunistic drives. These are essentially here today and gone tomorrow. Several hundred pheasants are feeding in a fast diminishing block of carrots, within easy flying distance of a main covert, a fall of woodcock arrives in the night, a thousand geese turn up on that flooded lower meadow. For the shoot manager who is quick on his feet, these all provide scope for opportunistic drives.

Having clarified in his own mind which drives need to be shot sooner, and which are likely to be equally effective later in the season, the shoot manager now addresses the specific choice of drives for the opening shoot. The old formula regarding early season drives was 'shoot the boundaries'. There is every likelihood that your shooting neighbours will also do just that and this tends to leave one with little choice. If the birds on your side of the fence suddenly notice distinctly less crowding next door, there is more than a passing chance they will gravitate in that direction, just in time to get shot by your neighbour as he shoots his boundaries again a week or so later.

After walking the main drives, the shoot manager should be able to get a good idea of what to include in his first day's shooting. That day will typically comprise seven drives. To cope with this sort of programme the shoot manager should think in terms of short-listing ten drives. As he walks the drives, or soon after, the shoot manager should personally supervise the placing of gun number pegs for each of those ten drives. Getting pegs in the right position is an important aspect of shoot day management which tends to get overlooked. All too often pegs get put in *roughly* the right place, guns are told to 'move about' if birds seem to be going too far one way or the other. This is not only a bad and slovenly practice, but it is potentially dangerous. The extra effort to get things just right is not excessive, it is well worth while. When placing gun pegs, it is always questionable whether they will still be standing a week or so later as domestic and wild animals share a penchant for flattening the sticks and eating number cards. A shoot manager has to find out what survives best in his locality. Start with a simple stick and card approach, then thicken up the pegs to broomstick thickness. If they still get knocked down, try short, fat plank-like pegs with painted numbers. It takes a small elephant to knock these over and there is no number card to eat!

Most shoot managers number the gun pegs from right to left when facing the drive. This means that gun number one is on the extreme right and guns 8, 9 or 10 on the extreme left. However, because the world is full of individuals, some do it the other way around. It really matters not which way you number, but do be consistent and do tell guns which way things are numbered at the start of the day. Overweight and unfit guests do not always appreciate the therapeutic benefits of hastening two hundred unnecessary yards across heavy plough. On learning that their actual peg is some distance removed in the opposite direction, as a result of numbering confusion, they have been known to get disgruntled.

The almost final decision as to which drives to include in the first day's shooting will be taken the day before that event. Especially when harvesting, cultivation or other field work is in full swing, key local farmers must be spoken to at this eleventh hour. A shoot manager looks a bit foolish when he starts to line up guns facing a field in which a cheerful army of potato pickers are noisily at work. It matters not that when he saw the place yesterday it was quiet as the grave, and walking with pheasants; someone should have found out what was in store.

Some weeks before the new shooting season starts, a view is taken regarding beaters. Are they really needed? If so, how many and from where do they come? Recruiting beaters is very definitely not a job for the shoot manager, that is unless he happens to have an available squad of estate workers who can be pressed into service. A full time keeper is ideally placed to review the local pool of potential beaters, also to reject or omit all those with criminal records or poaching inclinations. In the absence of a full time keeper, the proposed head picker up, proposed head beater, or some other trustworthy local individual, should be given the job.

In some parts of Britain there is enough formal shooting for semi-professional beaters to make a winter living. Goodness knows what they do all summer but from September onwards it is a case of 'have dog and stick, will travel'. All beaters are now expensive; the times when men got a brace of pheasant for the day, and boys got half a brace, are long gone. Outside of the semi-professionals, who know how to behave, when to be quiet, when to tap sticks and so on, most of those who volunteer as shoot beaters, are scarcely worth a day's wage.

The management problem when dealing with fickle casual labour such as beaters, is to get the right number of able bodied men or women on the right day. If too few turn up, the driving programme may have to be curtailed – a 'can't shoot the big wood without twenty beaters' type of situation. If too many turn up, the shoot manager usually has to dig deeper into his pocket and pay them. It is doubtful wisdom to turn away beaters who arrive for a day's shooting. Send them away today and they may not be around tomorrow when you really need them.

Most beaters need to be paid in cash. Shoot managers who do not customarily walk around with largish sums in their back pockets, need to think about this a day or so ahead. The situation can be eased by the fact that game dealers tend to pay in cash but such monies will not however, be around until well after the beaters have gone home. Where double days of shooting are planned, game money from day one can be used to pay beaters on the next.

Some shoots get by without any paid beaters at all. The usual formula here is to collect together a band of volunteer beaters: wives, girl friends, children and anyone else who can be persuaded or coerced into so doing, crash about in the undergrowth in the good cause of shooting. All may go well in the early part of the season; as weather deteriorates, woods get wetter and land more muddy, volunteer beating groups tend to dwindle in size.

Volunteer beaters are usually marshalled and led by a volunteer Head Beater. This person does not beat heads but can give the impression that he or she would like to. They often fail to appreciate that if you employ volunteer beaters, they *will* make a hash of the odd drive. Also that if one is over officious and bullies those wives, girl friends and the like, there will be fewer volunteers next week!

A few shoots dispense with paid beaters by having two complete teams of guns, divided into an A team and a B team. The toss of a coin decides whether A or B shoot first. The losing team then puts down its guns, scrambles into extra waterproofs, takes up sticks and beats for the first drive. When that is through, a flurry of dressing and undressing takes place as the teams change over. Bearing in mind that a typical day's shooting is seven drives, one of these two gun teams usually gets short-changed. The A and B team approach has its enthusiasts, goodness knows why.

As the shoot manager puts finishing touches to his proposed first day of shooting, a certain balancing of conflicting interests has to be borne in mind: guns want to shoot as much as possible; keepers want them to shoot as little as possible – at least early in the season; beaters want to get paid as much as possible for doing as little as possible.

Farmers are wary of vehicle damage to fields, foresters dread damage to trees and churned up tracks, cottagers pray for that semi-tame pheasant in their back garden, shoot managers fear that everyone will be dissatisfied before the shoot day is over. Maintaining a subtle balance between expectation and realization, is the surest way of keeping most people happy, most of the time. Only God can look after that tame pheasant!

If guns only expect a moderate day, they are delighted when things go better and birds fly high; when beaters expect to work a full day, they are pleased if the day finishes early, and not disgruntled if it doesn't; if farmers and foresters half expect damage, they are cheerful when this is kept to a minimum. The need for diplomacy, public relations and man management reaches a peak at the start of the shooting season.

Dogs can bring joy and pleasure to a day's shooting; they can also be a curse. Those which belong to pickers-up, beaters or other paid helpers are easily dealt with: if they transgress or have anti-social tendencies, they can be banished. If old Fred does not go beating without that crossbred bull terrier, so be it. Last year it caught a fox in a bramble patch and slew it single-handed and this was a notable point in its favour. Since then however, it has attempted to repeat the process on two dogs in the beating line; it also severely bit the hand of its loving owner as he intervened in one such fight. Old Fred and his dog are best beating elsewhere.

It is dogs that belong to guns or to local friends who pick-up on a voluntary basis, which often cause the shoot manager most hassle. Far too many owners see their dogs as paragons of virtue, the fact that they are *quite* well trained makes it worse. Confident that Jake, Fred and Susy will not run in or run off, some owners decline to keep them on leads or peg them for drives. A large fallow deer barges out of the wood ahead, and gallops through the line of guns; it then heads for that wood down the hill which is the next drive. Like one, the trio of dogs set off in hot pursuit and by the time they are eventually retrieved that wood down the hill is off the list of drives for the day. Everyone is embarrassed and apologetic, 'He has never run off like that before,' is the usual comment. The fact is that Jake, Fred and Susy have probably never had a wild deer rush past them like that before. Probably half the field trial dogs in the country would have taken off in such circumstances, but that does not stop a drive being ruined for that day. When a shoot manager, with his intimate knowledge of the local situation, feels there is any risk of dogs spoiling drives, he should ask for them to be put on leads. As a general rule, most dogs are better pegged, or held by someone, during drives.

Transporting guns and beaters about the shoot used to be simple matter. A weatherproof trailer with straw bale seats, or a horse box, van, lorry or whatever, was laid on for the guns. A similar wagon – probably less well stocked with hot soup and drinks – accommodated the beating fraternity. It all worked very well. The 'gun bus', 'battle wagon' or whatever the gun transport was called, and the beater wagon both had similar ground speeds. There was a good balance which enabled guns and beaters to arrive in their respective positions at about the same time.

Much has now changed. On a growing number of large shoots, guns now cruise from drive to drive in a fleet of cross country vehicles; this is splendid for the business man with a mobile telephone on board as it means he can talk to his office and business colleagues in between drives. The practice does however present the shoot manager with a recurring vehicle marshalling problem. As eight Range

Rovers or whatever discharge people and dogs in a narrow country lane, there is potential for noise in general and door slamming in particular: this does not improve the drive, shortly to commence

The other problem is that, on the far side of the wood, the beaters' trailer is slowly churning its way along muddy tracks and it will not reach the beater start-point for another quarter of an hour or so. Everyone else hangs around and gets cold (or goes back and telephones the office again). When guns use cross country vehicles which move them around the shoot quickly, beater transport systems needs comparable uprating.

Back at the Range Rovers, the shoot manager wanted to have a brief word with the guns about some aspect of the next drive. In a 'gun bus' situation he could have said it once, now he has to repeat the message half a dozen times and even then someone fails to hear. A peahen which has lived in that particular wood for two years may now get shot.

One final point regarding the transportation of guns. When a single communal wagon is used by all guns, plus friends or wives who are picking up, people get to know each other and a spirit of camaraderie develops. This cannot and does not occur to the same extent when a multiplicity of vehicles is used for the job.

Those who are going to shoot on a particular day will have been notified some weeks ahead. The date, meeting place and start time will all have been specified. When they are guests shooting at a place for the first time, the shoot manager will have ensured that all were told what type of shooting to expect, also how formal or informal the day was going to be. If for instance, the game plan is to walk up salt marshes all morning, it is probably not a good idea to wear a decent shooting suit. Everyone – guests and home team alike – should aim to be at the start point, booted up and ready to go, at least a quarter of an hour before the scheduled start. It is not only bad manners in the extreme, but also inconsiderate, to be late on such occasions.

The final decision regarding which drives to include in the day's programme is usually made around breakfast time on the shoot day. As he walks across to meet the guns the shoot manager – or shoot captain as he may be termed on such days, is wise to have two white cards in his pocket. The first card lists all drives planned, the likely order, and the two or three spare drives which have been pegged. There is space alongside each drive for a running total of birds shot, to be added as the day progresses. The keeper had an identical card to this an hour ago; his is now covered in signs and strange hieroglyphics to remind him of critical things in each drive – like getting his 'stop' man in place for drive four, *before* starting drive three. Also getting a picker up in place, across the river, for drive two; and so on. The second white card carried by the shoot manager is an *aide memoire* covering all points he wants to include in his pre-shoot chat. Introductions are first on the agenda and the names of all those expected to shoot will be listed on the card.

Some people will know each other, some will be strangers. The shoot manager breaks the social ice, and newcomers shake hands. Food and drink plans are spelled out, so everyone knows what to expect. A summary of drives planned for the early part of the day is given to the assembled guns with an indication of what is in store after that. Some shoot managers issue a fixed drive programme at this point. This approach indicates good preparation, but if drives are mentioned by name it does not facilitate close control over numbers shot as the day progresses.

Gun peg numbers are now drawn using ivory pegs, paper numbers in a hat, or a prewritten drive card with drive numbers not names. The method of peg numbering is explained, i.e. right to left, also how guns change numbers from drive to drive. The usual way to change numbers is to add two after each drive; this means that number one moves to number three and then to number five peg over the first three drives. The only drawback of this method is that a gun shoots with the same two neighbours all day. To make life more varied and exciting, some shoots have more complex number changing routines; odd number moving up two, and even number moving down two with each successive drive, is one such alternative. This format is certainly exciting, but, after two or three drives, half the guns don't know where to go. Frantic finger counting, plus 'take away the number you first thought of' seems to become the order of the day. To restore order to chaos at such times, the shoot manager must, at the very outset, mark on his own white card who drew what number at the start of the day. It then only takes a few seconds to sort out later difficulties. Prewritten drive cards make life easier for the less numerate.

Signals for starting and ending drives will be clearly explained. Where possible the shoot manager will arrange that gun signals and keeper signals involve different instruments. In this way confusion is less likely to occur, as when half the guns thought that a particular whistle means the end of drive but in practice it called for beaters to push out the last bit of cover. The simplest approach is for the shoot manager to use a horn and the keeper and his team, whistles.

Some shoot managers like to start the drive by firing one shot. In gales or storms this may be necessary but on most normal days, an individual with healthy lungs can produce ample noise from a standard shooting horn. A hunting horn note travels even further when blown by those who know how.

A word on spent cartridges does not go amiss. These are, after all, litter, look unsightly and can be harmful if eaten by livestock. When walking across rough countryside, it is neither easy nor practical to scrabble about for empty cases. When standing by a peg on a lowland drive however, it takes minimal effort to pick up those spent cases after the drive. Put them in a spare pocket and tip them into a box or some other container back at the vehicles.

What can be shot, and when, is the next point for discussion and here the shoot manager must be as precise as possible. It is not good enough to say 'we shoot everything but hen pheasants' or some such generality. For reasons of safety, a growing number of shoots now opt for no ground game shooting at all. This certainly resolves the hare, rabbit and muntjac question, but what about foxes? Where birds are concerned, all those which are likely to be seen, should be mentioned. Any ornamental pheasants, guinea fowl, white pheasants or whatever, which are definitely *not* to be shot must be mentioned now.

The final heading on the shoot manager's *aide memoire* card says 'safety'. Firearms are undeniably dangerous. Mix people with guns, add the spark of excitement, throw in dogs, fences, ditches, old pieces of machinery and whatever else may ensnare the unwary foot, and you have potential for an accident. Anyone who resents being reminded of the danger from low shots in front, swinging through the line, or of richochets from stone walls, clipped hedges, straw stubble and even water – should probably not be in that shooting party. Strict enforcement of a 'no loaded guns and no shooting between drives' policy is essential.

The last words on the shoot managers card remind him to 'Be Clear. Be Brief. Ask for questions'.

All this chatting has taken five minutes or so. Guns are now given a few minutes to climb aboard vehicles. The shooting party then moves off to the first drive of the new season.

7 : *The Shooting Day*

An opening drive sets the tone for the whole day's shooting. It does not need to be big; it does need to be impressive. It should provide as much shooting as possible for as many people as possible, as quickly as possible.

Those with good shooting on their doorsteps are few and fortunate. For most, a day spent with gun and dog entails a fair amount of travel. By the time today's party assembled at the keeper's cottage, some had been travelling since crack of dawn, others had arrived the previous evening, and had stayed locally overnight. All need to be stimulated. The first drive should be like a child's skyrocket. It should go fizz, then whoosh!

First drive today is a small wood called Sicily. It sits close to the 'toe' of a long, thin, riding-boot shaped stand of timber, called Italy wood. Sicily is no more than five or six acres in extent. To outward appearances it is a normal unpretentious looking wood, whose core appears to be dense pines and a lot of rhododendron bushes; mature oak and beech surround the perimeter. The secret of Sicily lies in its history, as this piece of land was the site of a fortified manor house. All structures have long since crumbled, cut stone and heavy beams carted off for incorporation in other buildings around the district, rubble taken to build up roads and harden trackways. All that remains of a once great establishment, are the defensive moats; deep and canal-like, fringed with reeds and overhung with bushes, these old moats still surround most of the site and bisect it in the middle.

No pheasants or duck are ever released into Sicily. It is, however, one of those bits of countryside which attracts game like a magnet: pheasants from Italy wood leach into there faster than the keepers would like; wild duck, scouring local stubbles and potato fields by night, lie up here by day. As the first frosts of winter lay an iron hand on the countryside, Sicily becomes a great place for woodcock. At all times, it is noted for shoot day pyrotechnics.

The place has to be approached with great care; vehicles are parked two hundred yards away; the shoot manager asks that all dogs be put on leads. 'No talking.' Two guns have gone with the beaters and will stand on pegs at the rear of the wood; they may have some testing shots.

The remaining guns are led quietly to their appropriate pegs. As he places each gun, the shoot manager indicates to those who have not shot here before, from which direction birds can be expected; this may seem logical, but it is not always done. If all early birds are likely to come from the left, and late ones from the right, a gun needs to be told this interesting piece of news. Granted, he will find out in due course, but by that time he will have completely failed to see some opportunities through gazing fixedly in the wrong direction.

The horn is blown to start the drive and an answering whistle from the back of the wood and a clatter of sticks indicates that beaters are on the move. Within minutes, further whistles in the wood indicates that birds too are on the move. A dozen wild duck appear, climbing steeply over the beech trees. They see the guns and swing right handed crossing the centre of the line, a full gunshot up. The subsequent volley of shots decants several dozen pigeons and they come bursting out through the trees in all directions. More mallard are on the wing, a party of teal circle higher and higher over the centre of the wood, pheasants now begin to appear. Their initial reaction was to run before the beaters, but in this wood, stretches of water act as natural flushing points. In a series of waves, pheasants of all sizes break cover. A lone woodcock effects a cunning escape – it flies straight between two guns at head height. As they turn for the shot behind, it lines up on the shoot manager's vehicle and makes a beeline for that, at windscreen height. No one shoots. In the closing seconds of the drive a disorientated flock of mallard cross the line of guns from behind. They are obviously heading for the peace and quiet of the moats! One of that number goes into the bag.

The horn blows, guns are unloaded. Sicily drive has lasted less than ten minutes, everyone has pulled a trigger. Not all have shot straight, but twenty or so birds seem to have been accounted for. On the grass and stubble which surround this wood, the pick up is quick and easy. One of those last duck was seen to crash-land in the moats. Beaters seem reluctant to try and retrieve it. The previous season one of their number waded into a moat on such a mission and promptly got stuck fast in evil-smelling mud. When onlookers realised the seriousness of his position a rope was quickly fetched, but the man had sunk up to his waist by the time that came and it took five strong men to haul him out. The picker up with his two dogs goes off to collect the duck. He has a van – which doubles as game cart on shoot days, he knows where the next drive is, he will catch up. Guns walk back to vehicles with a spring in their step, chatting avidly. They have indeed been stimulated.

The balance of drives that morning are boundary game strips. As the shoot manager prepares to start the second drive, the picker up arrives from his duck collecting errand. He gives an exact tally for the first drive which the shoot manager notes on his white drive card: twenty-four head, half of them pheasants. Those birds will by now be braced and hanging in the game cart not lying around in heaps in the beater wagon or in the back of assorted vehicles.

Today's shoot plan calls for two hundred birds which means about thirty head per drive. From a mathematical viewpoint the first drive was a little below par:

from a practical viewpoint, it matters not the slightest, as there is ample time to catch up on numbers. Sicily provided the fizz and whoosh that were needed.

As the day progresses some drives go better than expected, others worse. Pheasants that were laboriously encouraged to walk up-hill to the Jerusalem artichokes, fly predictably well. Those artichokes have been there for three years. Patterns of bird behaviour on this drive seem fairly constant, year on year. By comparison, one newly planted strip of kale caused all sorts of problems. In the first half of the drive, most birds flew back over the beaters' heads, the remainder surged to a bend in the kale and broke out over one gun with a mighty roar of wings. Not what was expected and the approach here will obviously need to be changed.

The horn blows to end the fourth drive. Those guns with dogs put them out to retrieve, the dog-less pick up all obvious birds and lay them by their own gun peg. They wait to advise whoever is picking up regarding any other birds. On such occasions it is simply not good enough to say casually 'three in front, two behind' and walk away: a picker up needs coherent information if he or she is not to waste a stack of time searching unnecessarily in the wrong places. What a picker up likes to hear is a succinct statement like: 'Three cock pheasants in front, all in, or close to, that big thicket. Two birds behind in the tussock grass. A woodcock close to and a hen pheasant well back.' Guns should not need reminding that if, by accident or design, they or their dog pick up a bird shot by the next door neighbour, it should be handed back to that individual with a 'your bird I believe' comment. If that neighbour is busily retrieving elsewhere, his bird should be laid by the appropriate gun peg, especially if it is a woodcock.

With most birds collected, and pickers up duly briefed, it remains only to gather up spent cartridge cases, and head for vehicles. With any luck lunch will follow.

There are conflicting views on how and when shooting parties are best fed. Main protagonists are the 'stop for lunch' brigade and the 'shoot through' contingent; defections from one camp to the other are rare indeed. The main advantage of stopping for lunch is that shooting party members with regular eating habits, who have breakfasted early, are not subjected to the discomfort of waiting too long for their next meal. A secondary, but not unimportant advantage of stopping for lunch is that two or three hours of exercise in the afternoon is a natural antidote to any over indulgence at lunch time.

The disadvantage of stopping for lunch is that it requires considerable liaison skills between those in charge of shooting and the catering establishment. Whether it be a cold picnic on moor or stubbles in September, or hot meal in lodge hut or pub in December, it has to be ready on time. Only in this way can the lunch break be kept to an acceptable timescale. One hour's duration is the ideal to aim for; when shoot lunches take too long, the afternoon programme has to be curtailed, also beaters tend to get restless at being kept hanging around. The possibility of birds not having enough time to settle down, feed and get to roost before short winter hours of daylight run out, can be another by-product of overly long lunches.

The main advantage of shooting through is supposed to be that an early finish gives the birds that extra hour to settle down before darkness falls. In practice, a lot of shoot-through enthusiasts continue shooting every bit as long as the stop for lunch brigade. For those who like to eat in a thoroughly leisurely manner, the shoot through approach has obvious attractions. The disadvantages of shooting-through are that many of these delayed lunches don't start until 4 p.m. and end around 6.00 p.m. By this time, the combined effects of an early start, ample exercise and a long day, followed by a relaxing meal in a warm room, begin to take their toll. Keeping awake for two hours, driving home over frosty roads, is not as easy as it seems. When a gun does arrive home he is frozen stiff from driving with the heater off and the windows open. The last thing on earth the shoot-through enthusiast then feels like doing is going to that important dinner party, which he agreed to attend three weeks ago!

With private shooting parties, the personal whim of the host or shoot manager, dictates the lunch decision. With syndicates it becomes a committee decision, with opposing camps lobbying for support as voting time draws near. With commercial shooting parties, there is no choice. You stop for lunch.

This party is fortunate, they stop for lunch! An hour later, the keeper and picker up arrive at the lunch hut. The shoot manager announces 'ten minutes warning' to assembled diners, then disappears outside to review plans for the afternoon. The morning tally stands at a hundred and forty head, well on the way to that quota of two hundred head. So well on the way, that, unless changes are made, planned numbers could be exceeded by quite a margin.

Controlling numbers and influencing the quality of birds on shoot days, are two of the hardest tasks which confront the shoot manager. They often seem thankless tasks; get it right and success is taken for granted; get it wrong and discontented grumbling is never far away.

The shoot manager who is unwilling, unable or plain uninterested in controlling numbers on easy days such as this, early in the season, makes a rod for his own back. It can be used to beat him on lean, cold days of late December and January. Three drives were pre-planned for this afternoon and there are three pegged drives in reserve. The shoot manager is reluctant to change his last drive of the day; just as the first drive sets the tone for the day, the last drive puts a seal of success on the day. There are only a small number of good first drives on most shoots and good last drives are equally scarce. The first drive should be short, sharp and impressive, 'fizz and whoosh'. The last drive should be similar, but with a 'bang' to end the day.

The first two drives planned for the afternoon can be changed without any problems. One of the reserve drives has a question mark over it. When the shoot manager and his keeper walked the place a couple of weeks ago, it seemed sparsely populated with pheasants; the evidence of grain consumption at feed points seems to endorse this view. There is a danger that the drive may be a flop, so now is as good a time as any to find out. Also, while walking the land on that pre-shoot excursion, it was noticed that three good coveys of wild partridge were in evidence on the old racecourse. That piece of land is presently fringed by a large field of carrots and other game is likely to be around. With no further ado it is decided to walk the carrot field and racecourse immediately after lunch. The questionable reserve drive will then be tackled. The day will finish with the pre-planned last drive.

Members of the shooting party are by now pulling on boots and generally stirring themselves for action. They are given 'five minutes warning' and told they are walking after partridge for the first drive. All seem cheerful about this news, except the man with a damaged leg. He is told that the picker up is waiting to take him to the extreme end of the drive, where he will be a solitary standing gun. It is impressed upon him that his performance will be watched with interest by all who are walking!

The carrot field and racecourse drive goes well; half a dozen old cock pheasants are found lurking in the carrots, the party makes good contact with two coveys of partridge. A third covey retreats ahead of the gunfire and advancing line of people, stops midway down the racecourse, then sweeps forward again, straight over the standing gun. Two shots ring out and the covey continues unscathed. One suspects that a certain lame gun will be reminded of that feat before the day is out!

The second drive after lunch is a quiet affair, rather as expected. The last drive crackles and bangs and end the day on a high note. With the last drive over, guns head back to the assembly point from which they started that morning. Tea may, or may not, be on the agenda.

The keeper now has two immediate tasks. Firstly to pay off the beaters, so they are kept hanging around as little as possible. Secondly to organise the game lay out. The time was when a game layout was *de rigeur* for all shoots. It could be in the game larder itself, where such a place existed close to the scene of shooting. At other times game was laid out on the ground or perhaps along a railing fence. Some modern keepers baulk at the work to get birds laid out, and the time to collect them up again afterwards. Shoot managers are not unknown who condone this idle approach, and the game layout gets omitted. Most people who have been shooting for the day like to see a good layout. Continental guns, if they are in a position of influence, will insist on it; Germans in particular, but also Dutch, Belgium, Danish and some other sportsmen from northern climes are firm believers that game shot during the course of the day, be given a musical salute. Hunting horns are produced, hunters stand respectfully to one side of the game. A series of 'calls' are then sounded, one for each game species present, a sort of Last Post for pheasants, Last Post for duck and so on. This is the time when short speeches of thanks are made, to shoot manager and host.

As he clears away the layout, the keeper and one or two beater stalwarts, who usually stay behind to help, check each bird for wing tags. This shoot put all tags on the left wing when it turned birds out to covert. There could however be birds from other estates present, so both wings need to be checked. All tags retrieved are collected by the keeper and put safely away. These tags have a story to tell as the season unfolds. While clearing the layout, the keeper selects an appropriate number of the best birds to be given to the guns. Many such birds will have to travel in the back of a vehicle for several hours, befor arriving at a suitable larder, so the keeper makes a point of selecting cold birds, shot earlier in the day, for this purpose.

Keepers need to be tipped at the end of a day's shooting; the shoot manager or host should advise all guns of the 'going rate'. If guns move off immediately after the game layout situation, there are no problems. The keeper goes around presenting a brace of birds to each gun and receives his tips as he goes. It is incidentally a nice practice for the shoot manager to offer any woodcock or unusual 'others' in the overall bag to those who shot them. If a gun declines this offer, fine. Hanging on to all the woodcock, just because game dealers clamour for them, is a spendthrift policy. Better far to be magnanimous in this small area.

Guns may not move off quickly, but stay around for tea or drinks. The keeper tip situation is then best resolved by one member of the party collecting the whole lot. This can be given to the shoot manager, and passed on to the keeper later in the evening. Meanwhile, birds for each gun are put in vehicles or left with the shoot manager. At all costs, the keeper must not be kept hanging around for his tips like a naughty schoolboy waiting for members of staff to emerge from the masters' common room. The keeper has dogs to feed and several pressing tasks – including a post mortem or debriefing chat with the shoot manager – before the evening is through.

Before guns disperse at the end of the day, the shoot manager must let it be known exactly what was achieved in terms of game species and numbers. By far the best way to do this is via a game card. These can be acquired from a number of sources; alternatively it does not cost a fortune to print up a few special cards for each particular shoot and some game cards are extremely attractive with pictures of game birds, country houses or something topical on the front. In addition to listing birds shot, the game card should list the full names of all guns present that day. Many people have personal game books which record individual shooting progress; days or weeks later when that game book is being brought up to date, it is all too easy to forget who was shooting when and where but with a game card tucked in the game book, all is revealed. The shoot manager usually has the job of filling in the game cards or he can produce one 'master card' and get the keeper or a helpful party member to write up the balance. Volunteer pickers up and non shooting guests who have been out for the day often welcome a game card: they should not be overlooked.

As afternoon slips into evening at the end of a shooting day, legs feel tired and minds lose their sharpness. Before that happens, the shoot manager and his keeper need to spend half an hour or so together. The first part of that meeting looks back at the day – a post mortem; the second half looks forward to the next day of shooting. Looking back, the shoot manager reports on how each drive

PLATE 9

The game cart: a good system being filled between drives.

PLATE 10

(*above*) Hare retrieved – unorthodox dog, classic style.
(*below*) Roadside poachers: this home-made silencer looks crude but works.

PLATE 11

Fox drive: an effective control measure in rough country.

(*left*) Fox wire in a vehicle track through sugar beet.

PLATE 12

(*below*) Hidden predator: pike have a notable impact on duck populations long before achieving the proportions of this 33 pounder.

seemed from the guns' point of view, the keeper then comments on what happened in the beating team, or was seen during that activity. Two mongrel dogs ran out of that kale strip which did rather poorly after lunch. They headed towards some tinker caravans which have been in a lay-by, close to the shoot boundary, for the past few weeks. It is more than possible that dogs have been frequenting the place and that could be why pheasant numbers are down so the keeper will talk to the tinkers about dog control. One 'stop' failed to get into position in time on another drive and some birds broke out sideways as a result of this; a more senior man will be given that job next time. Where birds flew backwards over beaters' heads, the problem could be tackled in several ways: extra stops, cutting a flushing strip in the kale, and so on. The easiest approach is to reverse the drive completely so the keeper will re-peg it accordingly.

Looking forward, the shoot manager has to decide what to include in that next shoot, in ten day's time. The keeper will 'have a stab' at pegging eight drives which the shoot manager favours. An 'almost final' decision regarding drives will be taken when shoot manager and keeper walk the land some day next week; a final decision will be taken after breakfast on the day of that shoot.

Controlling the quantity of birds shot on this opening day of the season, was an easy matter. It is not always so. Controlling the quality of birds presented is rarely easy. Even on the best of land, it does not take too many mistakes in the beating line for partridge to go running past guns in droves, rather than flying over them, also for supposedly high pheasant to come lurching forward twenty feet up in the air.

While a key job element of the shoot manager is to 'manage' the number of birds shot, it is absolutely critical that he does not appear to be gerrymandering. If guests or syndicate members get an inkling that they are being precluded from a particular drive because they might do too well, they tend to become gloomy or resentful. Any manipulation of the bag therefore calls for diplomacy and skill of a high order. Governing numbers down is a vastly preferable task to trying to boost them up.

It is slightly ironical that some of the obvious steps to reduce quantity can notably enhance the quality of birds presented. For instance, on a classic wood-to-wood drive situation, the distance which gun pegs are placed from the flushing wood, affects both quantity and quality. Normally placed gun pegs aim for a subtle balance between the quality of birds, and what the resident team of guns can achieve. Push the pegs back, and birds get higher and faster; fewer get shot, but those which do are that much more impressive. Advance the pegs to the very edge of the wood, and like as not, you will have a 'chicken shoot' on your hands. Changing drives from 'fat' to 'leaner' is a simple way of adjusting the score – as was done in the day reviewed. Speeding up the beater line may put the same number of birds over the guns but fewer get shot because birds come forward in flushes. Opening up the beater line, taking in only half the wood and/or missing out 'stops' so that birds leach out are all instruments of control. There is nothing unsporting about using them as needed, it is hard commercial sense.

The shoot manager's task is to provide guns with the day they expect. Nobody thanks him in the long run for overseeing a whopping great overshoot. The need to increase the scoring rate typically occurs when birds are scarce, conditions are bad or the team of guns cannot shoot straight.

When birds are scarce the only obvious antidote is to include more drives. A typical shoot has all sorts of spinneys and pit holes, many of which harbour a few birds. Some of these places are too small to include in a normal programme, but when need's must – include them. Ten drives on a short winter's day is eminently possible.

When weather conditions are seriously affecting sport, the shoot manager has to take a view. An impromptu coffee or soup break or even an early stop for lunch, is vastly preferable to getting guns and beaters soaked to the skin or frozen stiff. When conditions improve, birds fly better and guns usually shoot better.

It is when a team of guns are fundamentally lousy shots, that a shoot manager has his worst time. This situation will usually be apparent after the first or second drive of the day. The shoot manager should draw the party's attention to this fact, at that early point in time. He will no doubt add that, hopefully, they will soon get the measure of these birds. From that time onwards however, he is well advised to count, and record on his drive card, the number of shots fired per drive. He may choose to make marginal concessions with regard to moving guns forward. Under no circumstances however must he opt for the soft option, and oversee a chicken shoot; to do that is unethical, unsporting and a thorough waste of good birds.

In grandfather's day when guns shot badly, the trick was to stand a spare keeper or two behind the line, to help boost the score. Spare keepers are thin on the ground nowadays but if one or two of the weak party are seen to be better performers than the others, it can be useful to double-bank them behind the 'expensive seats' on each big drive. At the end of the day, if there are quibbles about low numbers shot, the revelation of how many cartridges were actually fired to achieve that poor result, will usually silence the critics!

Memorable days arise from a combination of factors. Some can be planned, others are pure chance; there is no magic formula. Shoot managers who constantly strive to produce good days, who are prepared to be slightly unorthodox, who take chances which could leave them looking foolish, who grasp at opportunistic situations, are the individuals who invariably produce more memorable days than less adventurous fellows.

Halfway through a morning's pheasant shooting, a large flock of geese arrives in the district and pitch into a field of sugar beet. An impromptu drive – ambush might be a better word – is arranged. Twenty minutes later a thousand geese, in lines abreast, fly straight over the guns, lined out behind a sheltered belt of trees. Fourteen casualties hardly decimate the geese, but every gun gets at least one. Most of those people had never before raised gun to a goose, let alone shot one and euphoria was still evident at lunch time, two hours later. That day was not forgotten in a hurry.

Variety of shooting is an important factor in its attractiveness. For this reason a shoot manager is well advised to ring the changes on his drives. If half the shoot involves snap shooting over rides in heavy woodland, and the balance high birds in open country, mix the drives up. Not more than two successive drives of the same type is a good working formula. This lesson has not been learned in Eastern Europe, nor it seems is the subtle difference between quantity and quality always appreciated. An American with extensive experience shooting in Britain, spent two days shooting pheasants in Eastern Europe. All drives were out of root crops: his summary comment was 'a thousand birds a day and not one memorable shot'.

Memorable shots for individuals are even more elusive than memorable days for whole parties. Many are fluke situations but that does not deter from their memorability.

A woodcock flew out of a belt of trees. As it crossed a broad dyke, it spotted guns on the far bank. It jinxed right, but was rolled over in the air. The next gun down the line sat glumly on his shooting stick, gun under arm, pipe in mouth. He had rather hoped that bird would survive to give him a chance, but no. The woodcock meanwhile looped through the air in his direction. Suddenly it became clear it would hit him on the head. In the last second, the seated gun casually raised one hand and caught the falling bird, inches in front of his face. Shooter and catcher raised their hats to each other, the drive went on. Those involved, and those who witnessed this scene, remember it well.

No one plans to shoot in a snow storm but such things occasionally happen by accident. When snow first starts to fall, especially for the first time in winter, pheasants can be galvanized by the experience. Standing on an exposed gun peg, in a blizzard of snow, while grey-looking pheasants hurtle past overhead is memorable enough. Actually shooting one or two heightens the experience.

8 : Poachers

What is a Poacher like? Ask the man on the top of that metaphorical Clapham omnibus and like as not, you will hear tell of some genial Victorian countryman. His trousers were tied with string below the knees, a ferret was in one pocket and purse nets in another. He pinched the Squire's rabbits by day and knocked over the odd roosting pheasant by night, when the keeper wasn't about. He was a colourful local character who did no real harm to anyone.

Such people did exist, and within living memory. That Lincolnshire poacher, about whom children sing, was perhaps one of them:

> When I was bound apprentice
> In good old Lincolnshire
> Full well I served my Master
> For more than seven years
> Then I took up o'poaching
> And what have I to fear
> For t'is my delight on a shining night
> In the season of the year . . .

Who can doubt this is a fine song, who can feel too aggrieved at that apprentice kicking over the traces? After all, the legendary Robin Hood was a poacher. For years he slew the King's deer in Sherwood Forest but everyone knows that he was good. By comparison, King John and his lackey the Sheriff of Nottingham, were both bad.

As they grapple with problems of poaching, present day shoot managers and their keepers must appreciate that public opinion is not wholeheartedly behind them, nor are those who enforce the law, nor, regrettably, are some of those who administer the Courts. Where poacher control is adjudged overly vigorous, there is more than a passing chance of the shoot being tarred with the same brush that blackened King John (who probably deserved it), also that Victorian Squire whose rabbits were being poached (who probably didn't). The man on the Clapham omnibus would be sadly disillusioned were he told that modern poachers ofter drive motor cars and shoot roadside pheasants from the window. Romantic mythology is more colourful than harsh reality.

There are two main types of poacher: professional and amateur. Professionals tend to be based in cities and are the heirs and successors to those Victorian poacher gangs, which sallied forth into the countryside to steal pheasants on a large scale. To counter such raiding, local keepers formed vigilante groups and when opposing forces clashed in darkened woods, the results were not very romantic: hand to hand fighting took place with cudgels, knuckledusters and knives. Blood was shed and limbs broken, men sometimes died.

The poacher gangs of today are equipped in a manner that would astound their grandfathers: high performance and all-terrain vehicles, spotlights, nets, dogs and a wide range of weapons. They make forays deep into the countryside, hit a target and are safely back in the anonimity of a city before daybreak. Flight is the preferred defence when trouble occurs but if cornered these gangs, like their Victorian predecessors, will fight viciously. Unless hankering after involvement in an 'OK Corral' type gun fight, a lone keeper is wise to get help before tackling such a gang.

Deer have become a popular target for professional poacher gangs. This is hardly surprising; half a dozen red or fallow deer carcases represent a lot of venison which, even on the 'dodgy game dealer' market, fetches a good price. It is easier money than knocking pheasants out of roosting trees or dragging nets across moor or heathland for grouse or partridge. Deer poaching is also conducive to hit-and-run operational tactics. Some of the deer poachers use rifles in conjunction with spotlights, which results in losing some injured beasts; others use buckshot, which has significant knock-down capability, but can also spoil the meat; yet others use long dogs or lurchers. For deer coursing, the lurcher fraternity seems able to breed large and formidable running machines; wolf hound and greyhound seem the predominant blood lines and resultant dogs can be the size of small Shetland ponies. Given any sort of open country, these specialist long dogs can run down, and throw down, a full grown deer with the ease of a greyhound catching a hare. It is also a silent process.

Amateur poachers are the heirs and successors of that Lincolnshire poacher. They no longer have string tied below the knees of their trousers, most don't work on the land. They tend to live on housing estates or in suburbia, and drive newish vehicles. They may be truck drivers or bricklayers, architects or publicans. Economic necessity has nothing to do with their poaching forays. They do it for excitement, and sometimes for greed; they are not visibly charismatic people. A majority of amateurs use shotguns or rifles, a few have long dogs, a minority use crossbows, catapaults, snares, traps and other less obvious ways of taking game.

Whether city professionals or suburban amateurs, all poachers need local knowledge to be successful. City gangs make a point of familiarising themselves with a district often by chatting with locals in the pub. Given half a chance they volunteer to go beating with the local shoot which is a splendid way to learn the lie of the land. Important aspects like where the keeper's house is located, where birds are concentrated, and the accessibility of major woods by decent tracks, all falls neatly into place as the shoot day progresses and at the end of which, they get paid for the work! Beating is, for the potential poacher, like visiting 'open to the public' country house gardens, for potential housebreakers: a heaven sent opportunity to 'case the joint', legally and in broad daylight.

When poachers get caught, it is fascinating to discover how they gained their the local knowledge. That long distance truck driver had been taking birds at night for years. Whenever his peregrinations brought him near the district, he stopped off for a bit of poaching. As a teenager he lived locally and he still knows local woods like the back of his hand.

An indignant man is caught running a lurcher. He cannot explain how a freshly killed hare happens to be in the back of his estate car. It turns out he has a brother-in-law, who lives locally.

The man who shot duck on the flooded meadows down by the railway, was very difficult to catch. No one knew where he came from or where he went; whenever the duck were in, he just turned up. In his case, a friend who drove trains on the local branch line kept an eye on the flooded meadows and gave the poacher a tip-off when duck were in. That poacher came some distance to shoot; he parked his vehicle by a railway bridge half a mile up the line, before walking down the track to the meadows. So it goes on – local knowledge every time.

Controlling this poaching is easier said than done. Main anti-poaching weapons available to the shoot manager and his keeper are: vigilance, precautions and toughness. Vigilance involves being constantly aware that poachers may be around somewhere on the shoot. Obvious signs to look for are: fresh vehicle tracks in places where there should be none; spent cartridge cases of a type not used by the keeper; game bird feathers by tracks or near roads. For instance, that patch of feathers in the stubble field would seem to indicate a cock partridge downed at speed: perhaps it clipped a power line or telephone wire – none around; perhaps a hawk slew it – no sign of carcass or remains; perhaps it was shot. There is a small public road forty yards away and on the grass verge are more partridge feathers, probably where poacher dog handed the bird to its owner.

Roadside poachers often work in groups of three in the following manner: one drives a vehicle at walking pace, the other two, with guns, walk the verges; their dogs work ahead of them, parallel to the slowly moving vehicle. They aim to flush game from the roadside, headland, hedgerow or near part of adjacent fields. When a pheasant or whatever jumps up, it is shot and quickly retrieved. Poachers then assess whether the shot has attracted attention; on this occasion a tractor driver over the fields seems interested in what is happening. The poacher trio jump into their vehicle, whistle up the dogs and drive off to another quiet road, five miles away.

Half the battle with poachers is to know what sort of people you are up against and how they operate. Once a shoot manager and his keeper know this, then with perseverance, most poachers will probably be caught and, given luck, they will be caught sooner rather than later. Running long dogs or lurchers by amateur poachers is a regional activity: they are the bane of some keeper's lives, others never see them. The long dog poacher traditionally works by night, using his dogs and nets to catch hares. He is especially effective in parts of the country where stone walls predominate, and hares run gateways from one field to another. Increasingly such poachers now seem to walk other people's moors and heaths in broad daylight, slipping dogs to course when the coast seems clear.

There is a motorised version of long dog poaching not unlike the technique used by the trio of roadside partridge shooters. Requirements for motorised coursing are a quiet road, open country and no roadside hedges or walls to obstruct the view. At an appropriate spot the poacher decants a lurcher (sometimes called a grule on these occasions) and a smaller dog, usually a terrier. The back doors of van or estate car are left open and the car drives slowly down the road. The grule trots along by the back wheel – limbering up – while the terrier scuttles about the road verge, headland, and near part of the field, looking for a hare. Up jumps a hare, off goes the grule and the course is on. When danger threatens the poacher whistles up his dogs, they jump aboard the moving vehicle via the back door, and their owner accelerates away. 'Just exercising the dogs' this operation is called, when you catch up with the speeding vehicle – its back doors still wide open!

Some shoot managers feel all this worry about vigilance is unnecessary. After all, they don't have a poaching problem. Perhaps they don't, not now. The first they know it has started, is when they run out of birds before Christmas.

A useful and very simple precautionary measure against poaching, is closely linked with vigilance. It involved taking the registration numbers of all vehicles seen in suspicious circumstances on or around the shoot. It is no bad thing for vehicle drivers to see that their numbers are being taken. That man with binoculars sitting in a newish Mercedes, may be a perfectly innocent bird watcher. If so, it matters not a jot to him if someone takes the car number. On the other hand, he may just be reconnoitering the land, with a view to himself or colleagues running vehicles or dogs there at night. If that is the case the Mercedes driver will appreciate the significance of number taking, and be unsettled by the experience.

For reasons best known to themselves, courting couples, parked close to pheasant woods, move off remarkably quickly when vehicle numbers are taken. Perhaps in the dusk with the light behind them, keepers and private detectives look not dissimiliar.

That farm worker on the tractor was indeed interested when he heard a shot, and saw the trio of roadside poachers collect a partridge. As a long-time beater and good friend of the shoot, he was one of the keepers' volunteer vehicle number collectors. That particular group sped away long before he was close enough to take the vehicle number. However, he was able to tell the keeper that they had a particular make of light blue van. Also that at least two of the dogs were liver and white springer spaniels. The keeper looked up his vehicles sighting records and found two sightings of a similar van and its registration number was recorded. He will now talk with the local police and try to persuade them to trace that vehicle and its owner.

Long distance truck drivers are not unknown to have poaching tendencies. They can be fearfully hard to catch as, by the nature of their calling, they are here today and gone tomorrow. A warning sign is when trucks stop overnight in remote parts of the shoot, especially if there is no driver asleep in the cab. Such a situation started to happen on one particular shoot. On three or four occasions an unattended heavy goods vehicle was found parked at night, in a lay-by, half a mile or so out of the village. The local keeper was convinced a truck driver was off poaching. An ambush was laid. In the early hours the missing driver returned and was pounced upon by the keeper and two heavyweight friends. Gasping for breath and scared for his life, the man was pinned down. They searched him for whatever he had been stealing but nothing incriminating was found. He had obviously hidden the birds and cleaned himself up, was the conclusion. No, no, protested the driver, with dread thoughts of kangaroo courts swimming into mind. He would explain all. He had been paying a visit to Mrs X in the village. Her husband was often away and she was happy to entertain her lover at such times but she insisted that he left his lorry well clear of the village in case the neighbours got suspicious!

Another precaution which can be used to good effect against poachers is nail boards. These are short thick pieces of plank with large nails banged through, laid in batches of four on tracks and in wheel ruts where unauthorized vehicles may drive. They immobilize a vehicle by puncturing several tyres at once. Their biggest impact is as a deterrent, when villains know they are in use. Old time poachers walked miles along ditches and in the shadow of hedges to get to a chosen wood. Modern poachers, whether professional or amateur, are firmly wedded to vehicles and they drive as close as possible to the scene of a proposed crime. The further away from that vehicle they have to travel, the less secure they feel. The prospect of having that escape lifeline severed, and a vehicle immobilized, miles from anywhere, is too fearful to contemplate. An old time poacher's fear of stumbling into a man trap, with the prospect of being deported to Botany Bay, could hardly seem worse.

Before deploying nail boards, it is of course essential, that all 'friendly forces' like local farmers and foresters, know where the things are laid. It is also important for a keeper to check them every morning, as he would a vermin trap line.

An old keeper had struggled for ages to catch one particular poacher, whose speciality was to slay pheasants at night with a crossbow. Vehicle marks, feathers and even the occasional crossbow bolt, were clear evidence of this nocturnal activity, but never a sight of poacher or vehicle. More and more nail boards got laid around the district, eventually the old keeper started to run over them himself, when he was not paying attention. At last the unexpected happened. There, one morning, was a modern red car, stuck in a wood with three flat tyres, and in the back were visible traces of blood and pheasant feathers. This was clearly the vehicle of his old enemy.

The keeper was beside himself with joy. Something had to be done before the owner returned and spirited his vehicle away. The keeper scuttled home for an axe and returned to the stranded car. When the car owner sneaked back later in the day with a couple of friends carrying spare wheels, he was startled by what he saw. His car had been converted from a saloon into an open top special – and none too scientifically either. Action such as this is, of course, totally reprehensible. No matter how provoked or angry they may be, keepers and/or shoot helpers *must not* take the law into their own hands and damage poachers' property.

When placing nail boards, it is advisable to ensure there is no obvious shoot property in the immediate vicinity. Newly stranded poachers get very excited. A release pen or keeper's hut is a good subject upon which to take revenge.

Trial bikers on heathland and moorland tracks may not steal birds but their presence can be very disruptive, especially in the nesting season. Nail boards on one moorland track obviously scored. The boards were subsequently found smashed to pieces and in addition, the disgruntled biker and his friends, had demolished thirty yards of dry stone walling. Revenge on their unseen assailant.

A precaution well worth taking on the shoot is to chain and lock all gates which lead to sensitive areas. There is no need for dozens of different keys, with all the trouble that entails, one master key can fit the lot. Shoot manager, keeper and chosen shoot helpers each have a gate key; the local farmer and forester are all given one to put on their vehicle key ring, just in case they need to open one of these gates. One small point: when a field gate is the type which readily lifts off its hinges, a chain will be necessary at both latch and hinge ends. Old gateways which are rarely used, also inviting gaps in hedges, through which someone might be tempted to drive, are best closed off with a post and wire fence.

A final and obvious precautionary measure against poachers, is high profile patrolling. With new shoots and new keepers, it is particularly important to start off as one intends to carry on. One shoot had more than its fair share of tinkers, diddicoys, or itinerants – call them what one choses. Now, although such people lurk in caravans by the roadside, they are to all intents and purposes urban dwellers. In times gone by they probably poached a bit of game but fortunately those rural skills have now largely been lost. The good news with tinkers is that game birds – except perhaps poults or release pen birds – are relatively safe. The bad news is, that nothing else is safe. If an item looks to have re-sale value and it can be cut down, dug up, dismantled or unscrewed and carried away by five strong men, some tinkers will take it. They are also enthusiastic emptiers of grain hoppers, to feed their own chickens, penned up behind the caravans.

Maintaining high profile keepering to deter tinkers is not as easy as it seems. As a keeper beavers about the shoot all day, the inhabitants of these caravans are all fast asleep. Like badgers, they rouse themselves at dusk, so the only way to make an impression on tinkers, who walk the place at night, is to do likewise. A newly installed keeper was aware of this and started to patrol regularly. Luck came his way when he stumbled upon two tinker youths at 3.00 am who were trying to carry off a feed hopper full of wheat and finding it very heavy. The keeper rushed at them with a blood chilling shout; he grabbed one, and his dog bit the other.

Both tinkers then escaped into the darkness. Within days, word was around that the new keeper was a madman with a savage dog, and that he roamed the place all night. Thereafter the local tinkers went stealing in less dangerous places.

Toughness is obviously linked with scaring the wits out of thieving youths. It does not necessitate beating the stuffing out of suspected poachers, though such things may happen. It does necessitate establishing a track record of positive action against poachers. If local police are prepared to co-operate and prosecute those caught poaching by keepers, so much the better. If they don't, the shoot manager should make a point of initiating several private prosecutions each year. On the face of it, this may seem both vindictive and a waste of money, it is neither. The value from prosecuting poachers lies not in the rather feeble fines which tend to be handed down by local magistrates but in local shock and in social impact.

Being hauled before a magistrate was traumatic for that man caught running a lurcher from the back of his estate car. To all outward appearances he was a law-abiding citizen. In one respect however, he was not law-abiding: he had been running his lurchers in this manner, and in various parts of the country, for years. He should have realized that one day his luck would run out. The local brother-in-law did not come out of this case too well: he must have known what was happening, thought the other locals. Why didn't he warn his wife's brother that the local shoot was tough on poachers? Here is where a policy of toughness pays off. Poachers need, and many have, local contacts. When quiet voices say to friends 'take care, poaching around here is dangerous', the shoot manager and his keeper are probably winning the poacher battle.

Most poachers aim to put bird or beast on a butcher's hook but a small minority deal in the live trade. This is a highly specialized area requiring knowledge, skill and daring of a high order. Above all it requires contacts, for this is essentially a 'steal to order' business. Widely quoted is the theory that reformed poachers make the best gamekeepers. Less widely appreciated, is the fact that lapsed gamekeepers make excellent poachers.

All poachers need some local knowledge. The man who plans to snatch stock birds from a laying pen, needs detailed local knowledge. He cannot risk motoring aimlessly around a shoot in the middle of the night trying to discover where the local keeper has hidden his stock birds this year. A Land Rover full of empty bird crates prompts interesting questions, a salmon landing net and a couple of spaniels on board does not help. The risks of this sort of business are not small, the rewards can be great. A couple of hundred stock birds delivered to the right person, can put many hundreds of pounds into the poacher's pocket, probably even more than the deer poachers get on a good night, and they have to split the proceeds more ways.

Stealing poults from release pens in late summer is a lower risk business. Release pens are more widely dispersed on most shoots, and that much less easily patrolled or protected. Again however, local knowledge is essential. The poult stealing poacher wants to strike as soon as possible after birds are released when the maximum number are still in the pen rather than in surrounding bushes.

Such birds are readily disposed of on the open market. The deer poacher or those shooting pheasants out of roosting trees are not safe until they get the game home. The live bird stealer is virtually safe, once he gets his vehicle back on the public highway, and a mile or two away from the estate he has robbed.

When a chance police roadblock stopped a Land Rover loaded with stolen pheasant poults in the early hours of the morning, things cannot have looked too good for the driver. But he helpfully explained how young birds were prone to heat exhaustion when moved at that time of year so moving them at night was the answer. Birds and driver went on their way. Disposing of stolen laying pen birds in spring and stolen poults in summer is surprisingly well organised. It is interesting to speculate on how that is achieved.

One very small section of the live game poaching market is concerned with hares which are destined for coursing. In the Irish Republic it is legal at certain times of year for licensed individuals to net wild hare for coursing. Some get chopped on the big day, a majority escape to run again. It used to be said that, at the Waterloo Cup Meeting at Altcar Meadows, most hares had Irish accents. One gathers they no longer ship in hares for that occasion, so where live hare poachers now sell their catch is anybody's guess.

The chorus of the Lincolnshire poacher's song goes '. . . it's my delight on a shining night, In the season of the year'. In these two lines the songwriter indicates a practical knowledge of poaching which may have been a little patchy. His reference to the season of the year is entirely right. Poaching is a highly seasonable business; it has nothing to do with legal seasons for taking game, everything to do with market prices. The poaching season for grouse probably starts in late July; this enables the black market to get birds to the big cities and into European capitals by 12 August, when fancy prices prevail. The season of the year for pheasant poaching is mid-October to mid-December. Prior to that there is no real market demand and birds tend to be small. After that, the market gets flooded with legitimately shot birds and prices tumble. Professional pheasant poaching is then no longer worth the candle.

The songwriter's reference to his delight being 'a shining night' is where lack of practical poaching experience may be apparent. Shining nights are usually still and quiet. A breaking stick can be heard a hundred yards away, a vehicle exhaust note, or sound of a gunshot, travels for miles.

Most poachers prefer the type of conditions which apparently prevailed at the start of the poem 'The Highwayman'.

> *The wind was a torrent of darkness*
> *Among the gusty trees*
> *The moon was a ghostly galleon*
> *Tossed upon cloudy seas . . .*
> *And a highwayman came riding . . .*
> *Up to the old Inn door.*

In such conditions, poachers can make all the noise they like without being heard.

Roosting birds are clearly visible against that cloudy sky, even if they are swaying about a fair bit.

Stories of bizarre poaching exploits are legion. Here is just one. A tall, black-bearded recluse lived in a provincial market town. Winter and summer, wet and dry, cold and hot, he always wore a long black overcoat and a black hat and walked with a stick. Sometimes the local children jeered at him, mostly he was ignored. He spoke to no one. Everyday at the same time he walked down to the river which flowed through the local park where he spent some time feeding the semi-tame mallard and other assorted duck. They did not seem to mind his weird appearance and always gathered around to be fed.

One day a passer-by noticed an interesting episode. As the duck milled about the old man's feet happily eating bread, a wire noose extended from the end of his walking stick. It slipped over the head of the nearest duck, a tug of the handle retrieved the wire and in one smooth move, duck and walking stick disappeared up under the overcoat. The other ducks continued eating happily, the old man adjusted his coat and walked off. When later he was visited by individuals following up the story, it was found that his cottage was almost wall to wall with duck feathers. He had been living off the park ducks for years.

9 : *Predators*

Mankind himself is said to be haunted by predators: gaunt, terrible and super-natural – the Four Horsemen of the Apocalypse. These grim riders, Invasion on a white horse, Civil War on a red, Famine on a black and Death on a pale horse, each has a mission of destruction. None who cross their path is spared.

The fourth rider has power over one quarter of the earth, with a right to slay people as he chooses. From time to time he appears to tire of this task. What better diversion and additional way of punishing mankind, than by destroying that which is preserved and cherished. Accordingly, Death's main weapons – pestilence and wild beasts – are unleashed against birds and animals that man would hope to shoot.

True or not, that is what it often seems like, from a shoot manager's point of view! As mentioned earlier, in those parts of France and much of the Irish Republic where preservation of game birds and organised shooting has ceased, miniscule numbers of game birds survive and there is visible evidence of rampant predator activity. It would not take many years for Britain to go the same way if lack of control prevailed. Game species that we are accustomed to seeing as part of the country scene would then virtually disappear.

So long as a reasonable proportion of land has keepering or game conservation of some sort, the problem is containable. Predators inevitably use unkeepered estates as breeding sanctuaries, but as numbers expand, overcrowding pushes them onto adjacent keepered land. The process of control needs to be like painting the Forth bridge: so long as it continues, all the time, things never get out of control. The relatively few keepered estates in the Irish Republic are typically surrounded on all sides by miles of totally unkeepered land. Controlling predators in such places, presents problems which King Canute would have understood.

Some gamekeepers are good at controlling predators, others very bad indeed. Predators fall into two simple categories: visible and invisible. Of visible preda-tors, birds are an obvious category, corvids taking pride of place on most shoots. Carrion crow and hooded crows (or hoodies) are closely related. Together they neatly divide the British Isles along some magical contours; hoodies take the hills, carrion crows everything else. Those in hooded crow country often claim that, in terms of egg and young game bird destruction, theirs is the worst predator of the two. They could well be right but one wonders whether this is a factor of the fundamental differences in the two species. Could it be that hoodies merely have less choice of food than their lowland cousins.

Both sorts of crow are first class nest finders and egg looters. Carrion crow like to use a lookout tree for this function. They do not find nests in the way humans do, by methodically searching likely places, but by watching closely the movements and reactions of all birds within sight of that lookout tree; they watch and watch and watch some more. Few nests escape past the egg laying stage; those which do tend to be tracked down once song birds start to shuttle to and fro on the nestling feeding run, or when game birds are escorting chicks. Hooded crows sometimes use a lookout tree or crag but also 'quarter' hill and moor to good effect. They particularly note how local birds respond to their presence. Anxious grouse or mobbing lapwing and curlews all indicate to a hooded crow that a nest or young birds are not far away.

Both types of crow are especially partial to ducklings. If a mother duck is unfortunate enough to be ambushed as she leads her newly hatched brood from nest site to local river, pond or whatever, an unpleasant massacre tends to occur. Crows are also very partial to game bird chicks which are particularly vulnerable during their first two or three weeks of life. Once they have flight feathers and can disperse like a covey of large bumble bees when attacked, the risk of a whole brood being wiped out is much reduced.

The size of birds which both sorts of crow can carry off is surprising. Pheasant, duck, partridge and grouse up to two or three weeks old are semi-immobilized, grabbed in one talon and removed. When working hedgerows and shrubberies, they will similarily snatch blackbird and song thrush fledgelings which are almost full grown. One of the few birds which tends to escape the attention of robber crows are mistle thrushes. They make bulky, obvious nests, well up in a tree and usually before there is much leaf cover. Their defence of that nest against corvids and raptors is so spirited that it is usually successful. Only a brave and determined grey squirrel has much hope of robbing a mistle thrush nest.

Birds of a feather flock together. From late summer and through the winter assorted corvids of the black variety often congregate in huge communal roosts. Carrion and hooded crows abandon their individuality for the night, and join with rooks and jackdaws in these gatherings. Lady Macbeth noted how '. . . the crow makes wing to the rooky wood'. They still do.

A crow roost on the shoot is hardly a good thing. It has been argued that come spring, they will all disperse. In the meanwhile, however, they will have doubled the consumption of feed grain in that part of the shoot, by robbing every hopper in sight. Furthermore they don't all disperse in spring; small groups of suicidal pioneers always seem to stay behind, hell bent on breeding in or near that comfortable roost wood.

When crow roosts occur, the best plan is to call together a few friends, give them a box of cartridges each, and make life hot for incoming crows early in the roosting season. They will soon get the message and move elsewhere. Crow traps of the aviary type can be kept operational all the year and they certainly help keep numbers under control.

A traditional methods of controlling corvids was by means of poison in eggs, which was undoubtedly effective, but is now illegal. Poisons can be used on the shoot *only* for control of rats, mice and moles, also grey squirrels in England and Wales. In Scotland, where a passable population of red squirrels still exists, the use of Warfarin type poisons against any squirrels is banned.

Not only are poisons illegal for use against birds, but so too are most narcotic and stupefying substances. Some very limited exceptions are made to the rule; these typically involve control of feral pigeons in city centres or around commercial grain silos, and for control of egg stealing gulls around tern nesting colonies.

Carrion crows and hooded crows have traditional nesting places. These are usually sited to give exceptional all round visibility: sitting crows do not like being taken by surprise. Corvids are extremely difficult to shoot off the nest; practically the only chance of so doing is on a wet and stormy night, when the sitting crow has its head down and is not paying much attention. Those who do find themselves under the nest of a sitting crow, must appreciate that the chances of shooting it through the nest with any normal sized shot are not good. If the first shot is fired into the nest, you only have one chance at the fleeing bird. Far better indicate ones presence with a shout or loud noise and have two chances. A departing crow often has a lot of height and a screen of branches to stack the odds in its favour.

When taking over a new shoot, the shoot manager should ensure that *all* old crow nests and magpie nests are physically demolished. Never mind the rook's nest. Knocking a hole in a crow's nest and leaving the superstructure in position is not good enough – an old nest can be repaired in double quick time and to all but detailed inspection, it still seems derelict. A brand new nest is there for all to see, if they but look.

Old crow nests are harder to dislodge than it might seem as a surprising amount of mud and roots get packed into the base. If there is a good clay soil locally, the centre of the nest becomes almost bricklike. Shooting them down with a great handful of conventional shot sized cartridges seems a waste. Alternatives are to use very heavy shot, or take a page out of the old keeper's book and melt some candle wax into a few cartridges to bind the shot. Your gunsmith may not approve, but it delivers an impressive punch at the top of a tall tree.

However hard one strives to keep on top of crows, they will always come sneaking back into the district from somewhere. One pair announced their presence by snatching a muscovy duckling from the shoot manager's stable yard. The plaintive peep, peep peep of the victim grew fainter as it was borne off over the trees, in a northerly direction. Now, everyone knows that the shortest distance between two points is 'as the crow flies'. Certainly when heading for home to feed their young, crows do not make many detours. Two small children who loved the ducklings witnessed this dastardly abduction. Swift retribution was promised and with gun in hand, the shoot manager marched north. He did not have far to go for within half a mile, a brand new crow's nest was spied in a traditional crow tree. From signs and sounds at ground level, there were obviously chicks on board. Two barrels of buckshot punched a wine bottle sized hole clear through the nest, simultaneously a lone crow squab was hurled out of the top of the tree, described a broad parabola, and crashed to earth. One gone, but how to dislodge the others. No sooner was the question asked than it was answered as two other sibling crows came tumbling through the hole in the floor of their lofty nursery. Two more shots took the side off what remained of the nest, the wind would shake out the rest. Mission accomplished, duckling avenged.

Where crow nests are not in desperately high trees, it is often possible to climb up to within ten feet or so, and knock them down with a long pole. Whoever does this job is advised to wear a hat, and motor-cycle or ski-goggles. The dust, filth and debris which tumbles out of an old crow's nest has to be seen and smelt to be believed!

Jackdaws are the commonest members of the crow family on most shoots. They are avid stealers of pheasant food and take eggs when they get the chance. Aviary-style crow traps are reasonably effective in controlling numbers. As with carrion crows, however, jackdaws just seem to keep on coming from somewhere.

Magpies and jays probably do more damage to song birds than to game birds; both are best controlled, both are difficult to shoot. Crow traps account for magpies but not for many jays. Magpie nests are robust structures with a roof of thorns, typically in a dense hedge but not very high up, so a long pole is often the best way to remove them. A jay nest looks thoroughly un-crowlike—more like that of a mistle-thrush; even sharp-eyed keepers find remarkably few.

Rooks are in evidence on many shoots. They are not as black in habit or personality as their feathers would indicate so most shoot managers tend to leave them be. If this is done, however, there is a tendency for rookeries to grow ever bigger. The best approach seems to be to cull some young rooks in early May. The old formula for keeping a rookery from growing was to take two young birds from each active nest, leaving one or two fledged young per nest.

Local people often have set ideas regarding the precise day that rook shoots must take place. The main requirement is that young birds be on the wing, but not fully fledged, so they can cruise around from tree to tree but cannot disappear to some great height, which is what the adult birds do when shooting starts. Rook pie enthusiasts, or those keen to experiment, will often take whatever gets shot; the best weapon is a .22 rifle. While checking a rookery with binoculars ahead of such a shoot, the author once found himself looking at a long thin neck and a head with a sharp bill, peering over a nest. There, in the very centre of a rookery, was a nesting heron, sharing the canopy of a great Scots pine, with no less than six pairs of rooks. Shortly after the rook shoot the herons hatched off and from then on there was a steady procession of parent birds going back and forth for food. Every time an incoming heron appeared in sight, a raucous cloud of rooks flew up to intercept and mob. The herons studiously ignored the rooky rabble, to land on their nest. As soon as they were down, all rooks would peacefully return to their own nests or drop back into the tree tops. It seemed as if flying herons were intruders but herons on that nest were honorary rooks. One can but speculate on how that particular relationship got established: probably the herons got there first in February, but lost their first brood.

Ravens are so thin on the ground that most shoot managers will never see one. Even on hills and mountains they are more likely to worry the sheep farmer than the gamekeeper. In Britain we are used to associating ravens with wild and desolate places but in parts of Ireland they nest in parkland trees, not unlike British carrion crows. Tower of London take note.

Raptors – hawks, falcons, owls and eagles – are all fairly visible predators. Some, like kestrels and tawny owls, may be present on a shoot all year, and breed locally. Others like hobby and peregrine falcon, winter in southern Europe or Africa but return in spring to breed. A whole spectrum of birds of prey are passage migrants, moving south through Britain in autumn en route from Scandinavia and Northern climes to Africa or the eastern Mediterranean. They move northward again in the spring. A few species, like short eared owls, stop over as winter visitors.

The impact of raptors on a shoot is to some extent influenced by the size of bird. Small ones like merlin or hobby have negligible impact, medium sized ones like kestrel and sparrow hawk can be difficult, big ones like peregrine, goshawk and harriers are difficult. At the two extremes, golden eagles are big but probably not all that troublesome, little owls are very small and can be very troublesome. Within Britain all raptors are fully protected.

The shoot manager and his keeper stand on their upland shoot. On the one hand they see a peregrine knock down a grouse, on the other a harrier quarters the moor in wavering flight – scaring the wits out of birds and small beasts. At such times there is always the danger that someone will get frustrated and unleash a shot in the general direction of hawk or falcon. The shoot manager must ensure this does not happen. The hills in Britain are not alive with the sound of music, they are alive with the sound of birdwatchers' boots. Impetuous acts by individuals can have far reaching and undesirable repercussions on shooting in general.

When open field rearing systems ruled supreme, kestrels were probably the gamekeeper's biggest single headache. Thousands of pheasant chicks scuttling about the grass in one small space attracted kestrel from miles around. Deprived of this temptation, kestrels today are reformed characters. There is no doubt that wild partridge chicks suffer a few casualties, together with some pheasant chicks. This damage, however, is hardly dramatic.

The kestrels replacement, as raptor enemy number one, for the modern gamekeeper on lowland shoots, is the tawny owl. The custom of turning out well grown pheasant poults into release pens plays right into the talons of delinquent tawny owls. There in the middle of the owl's home territory is an open topped release pen and in it are dozens of sleeping pheasant poults. Like terriers in a rickyard full of rats, owls take advantage of this sudden bonanza! One pounce, one tweak of its bill, and a poult is decapitated, then another, then another and so on. The sight which greets the keeper next morning is not attractive. Once a rogue tawny owl starts this poult killing routine, the only solution is to remove it from the district.

As a precautionary measure, in places of high owl attack risk, the shoot manager can consider investing in nets to roof over pens. This however is usually only possible with small pens and well nigh impossible with larger pens. In some parts of Europe the greatest threat to release pen poults comes from goshawks which have become remarkably prevalent, especially in West Germany. Not only release pens, but feed rides too have to be netted over, to stop pheasants of all sizes being snatched by these short winged angels of sudden death.

A goshawk migration corridor passed through the author's land. For two or three weeks every autumn and again in the spring, travelling goshawks were about. The first sign of a new arrival was when local wood pigeons and crows were seen flying along, five feet above the ground, on a clear and sunny day. For several years, a semi tame red-legged partridge had lived with assorted fowl in the stable yard. He was called partridge number one and his daily wanderings gave a fascinating insight into just how fixed in their habits mature game birds become. First thing in the morning partridge number one would be wandering along certain gravel paths and amongst the herbaceous border. By lunchtime he was out of view, somewhere down the paddocks. Later in the day – weather permitting – he dust bathed on the gravel drive. He then returned to the yard to strut about on the stable roof. If the weather seemed set fair, he spent the night in the lee of a stable chimney pot, in bad weather he joined chickens and ducks inside the stable.

Sitting on his favourite stable one autumn afternoon, destiny caught up with partridge number one. A feathered thunderbolt fell out of the sky and plucked him off the ridge of the roof. It then flew away without even stopping. From a graphic description of the incident, there was no doubt that partridge number one became a goshawk dinner.

Starlings are of course not predators. In summer they mind their own business and cause no trouble to anyone. In winter they have a predeliction to roost in chosen places, in massive numbers. For the most part, these nightly starling jamborees take place in big cities, much to the annoyance of city burghers and those whose buildings get targeted. Some starlings however opt for a more rural lifestyle and come autumn, a chattering and squeaking horde of birds descends nightly on some wood, spinney, copse or reed bed. Within a very short space of time, the whole roost site and the land beneath it, becomes so fouled with droppings that all other birds and animals quit the place. In this way 'starling power' can effectively neutralize a perfectly good pheasant covert. The antidote to starling roosts is similar to that for crow roosts. On this occasion, however, the group of vigilante volunteers chosen to move on the starlings, need to be equipped with dust shot or the smallest shot size available. Bangers alone rarely scare starlings away from a roost site, one has to get rough with them. The medicine may need repeating several times over a couple of weeks; after that the problem flies elsewhere.

Of four legged predators, foxer and feral cats are the obvious visible ones. Most of the others are to all intents and purposes, invisible. Signs that the invisible are around are there to be read like a book for those who know where to look.

Even gamekeepers who scarcely know the difference between a stoat and a pole cat, recognise that foxes are a threat, and try to do something about them. When dealing with foxes, there is the possibility of friction between a shoot and local hunt. Far too many keepers are of the view that fox hounds are nothing but bad news for shooting; if at all possible the hunt should be denied access to the land. From the other side of the fence, gamekeepers clearly spent most of their lives shooting, snaring and gassing foxes, wiring up gateways, and generally making the land impassable to mounted followers. This animosity is unfortunate, unnecessary and not in the best interests of either sport.

When taking over a new shoot, the shoot manager should, at the earliest opportunity, make peace with the hunt. Call on the Master of Foxhounds and work out with him how best the shoot and hunt can avoid treading upon each others toes. If the relationship has been bad for years, it will not flower and blossom overnight, but make a start. It is usually not too difficult for the hunt to try and avoid coming onto shoot land, at least until birds are well grown. Ideally this means not until well into November, by which time pheasants are fairly quick off the mark. Birds will not get chopped by foxhounds in the way that can happen when cubhunting hounds barge into a wood full of young pheasants in September.

When relationships between shoot and hunt are amicable, a new keeper or new shoot manager can accrue real benefits. The new keeper needs to know as quickly as possible the whereabouts of all fox earths and badger setts on the place; he also needs to know what lies just across his borders. Left to his own devices this could take many months. The people in the district who know all the answers are the local huntsman, and the hunt terrier man, and if they see the shoot as friends not enemies, their encyclopaedic knowledge of local fox and badger activities can be of great help. Whatever measures are employed against foxes the shoot manager should ensure his keepers do not destroy fox earths and badger setts. These places should be kept open and available for travelling predators. See a fox trotting along the side of that lower wood, and you know immediately where it will be based. Make a fox earth unusable and that travelling fox will create a new one which someone then has to find.

Foxes go to ground when hard pressed; they also breed in earths. Outside of this, many spend a large proportion of their time above ground, hunting by night and laying up by day. A clump of gorse on a sunny slope is a much favoured, fine weather location. Snaring is probably the most effective way of controlling foxes, as it not only keeps on top of the resident population, but also picks up travelling foxes. If things look good enough, some of the latter might always choose to settle down! A shoot manager should insist that his keeper has several dozen fox wires in place, on a semi permanent basis. A small number of those wires will invariably account for a majority of foxes caught. To snare any beast, a trapper needs to understand how each animal species lives, feeds, travels, what alarms it and what it accepts. The really good snarer works as much by intuition as to what is right, rather than what he can physically see, in terms of tracks, runways in the grass and so on.

When the hunt is known to be coming into the district, all fox wires should be immobilised for the day or lifted: this avoids bruising fox hunter sensitivities, and/or catching hounds, *but* all wires must be reset at the end of the day. Failure to do this can result in the shoot missing out on a fox catching bonanza as when hounds have thoroughly stirred up all foxes for miles around, there follows a significant amount of 'fox going home' traffic. Where a particular fox is marked to ground and its removal is imperative, the use of terrier and spades if often the best approach. That local terrier man will probably help if asked. Where the earth is not too extensive, Cymag is another alternative.

Feral cats are a problem for some shoots and not for others. They are particularly destructive when pheasant poults are at the release pen state. As with tawny owls, cats are inclined to go on a killing rampage when easy meat is around. For reasons which are not altogether clear, some feral cats grow far larger than their farmyard cousins. Where an organised programme of fox wiring is in place, this tends to account for marauding cats.

Invisible predators on the shoot are led by badgers. These animals have a quite remarkable way of keeping out of human sight. Time and again one hears from locals that there are only a few badgers locally; in reality, the place may be walking with badgers every fine summer night. Badgers are, of course, a fully protected species.

Ever since Kenneth Graham wrote *The Wind in the Willows*, badgers have been thought of as genial, wise and kindly animals. In reality they have a potential for villainy that water rat and mole would never have guessed! Badgers are extremely good at finding the nests of ground nesting birds and very partial to eating eggs. This applies not only to pheasants and partridge, but also to larks, pippets and others. Badgers have better 'noses' than the average fox. They also have very acute hearing which earns them many dinners on summer evenings.

Those who have hatched eggs in an incubator will know of the cheeping and peeping noises that come from within the eggs for a day or so before hatching. Badgers are highly sensitive to such noises and find a lot of their nests when eggs are just on the point of hatching. They are usually too slow to grab the sitting bird, but what matter, with all those eggs around. Small bird eggs are eaten whole. Pheasant eggs are eaten in the manner that a man eats boiled eggs! the top end is neatly bitten off, the chick is extracted.

When a badger, or more likely a family of badgers, stumbled upon a domestic turkey sitting on eggs in a nettle patch, they found a bird that was distinctly slow off the mark. Eggs and fifteen pounds of turkey were demolished on the spot. When the feast was over it looked as if a pack of jackals had eaten a whole deer.

Badgers share trackways with foxes, and not infrequently blunder into fox wires. A fox so caught panics wildly, badgers are more phlegmatic. They ponder the predicament, then usually set about digging up everything around and about which could be responsible for their enforced immobility. When the keeper arrives in the morning the fox is dead, the badger is very much alive. Releasing a disgruntled badger from a fox wire without being hospitalised by bites, or losing the odd finger, is easier said than done. In an ideal world the job is tackled by two people, but often it has to be done by one. Heavy duty gloves, of the type used when pruning roses or laying thorn hedges, are desirable; a short thick stick and wire cutters are essential; a nerve-free disposition is helpful.

Most badgers are unco-operative. They appear hell-bent not just on biting the hand of their human rescuer, but on biting it clean off. Before release can be effected, the animal has to be immobilized and this is where the stick gets used. The idea is to pin the animal's neck to the ground, which allows work to be done on the wire noose around neck or middle with the least risk of being bitten. Unfortunately, badgers don't have a proper neck – like some rugby prop forwards, the head is connected to the trunk by a wedge-shaped slab of gristle and bone. Despite this disadvantage and after some neat footwork, the badger is eventually anchored to one spot. With one hand, wire cutters are now slipped under the wire noose. With the other hand, the badger is grasped firmly by the tail. When the wire is snipped, the badger turns and lunges like a cobra at its rescuer. At this instant, the beast is hoisted bodily into the air by its tail. Only now does one fully appreciate the old saying about having a tiger by the tail. The inverted badger gyrates wildly with teeth snapping like a beartrap. This is the part that calls for the coolest nerve. The arm holding the badger has to be *exactly* horizontal. If it falls below ninety degrees, the badger bites its rescuer in the leg, lift the arm above horizontal and the badger bites him in the body somewhere under the arm; both are uncomfortable experiences.

After a few seconds at being inverted, the badger pauses to ponder his unusual position. A brave man may now put it down on the ground but he stands an excellent chance of promptly being bitten in the ankle. The logical thing to do is lower the badger into a steep sided ditch, or over a chain link fence, and withdraw rapidly.

Badgers are fast learners: once they have been in a fox wire and been released, they don't seem to get caught again. Farm cats also have an ability to remember such experiences. Most of the author's stable cats have been in fox wires at some time and subsequently live to ripe old ages, surrounded by woods full of fox wires, without repeating the experience. By comparison a hare once got caught in the same fox wire three times in five days. Twice it was released. On the third occasion, the fox for which the wire had been set arrived before the gamekeeper.

The mainstream of invisible predators on a shoot tends to comprise stoats, weasels, pole cats and mink. Secondary predators include hedgehogs, rats and the like. Collectively these predators take a larger toll of game species than might be imagined. The only really effective counter measures are tunnel traps and cage traps.

As with setting snares, some keepers are good at this sort of work; many are far from good. The performance of those in the 'grey' area between good and bad, can sometimes be enhanced and a session working with another keeper may be all that is needed. Ideally that more experienced man will then help the less able man actually set up his trap lines. Where keepers clearly lack ability in this area, the shoot manager should seriously consider employing a 'vermin man'. This individual gets provided with traps and wires, and paid a small retainer. After that his remuneration is based on what gets caught: so much per head, with possible premiums paid for species like mink.

Mink, ironically, are seen more often by fishermen than by shooting men or game keepers. Their negative impact on duck and waterfowl in a given waterway system is quite exceptional. Mink however are not all that difficult to catch in cage traps, by those who know how.

Pole cats – most of predominantly ferret blood – are more common and more widespread than many think. They are bloodthirsty little hunters and able to take noticeably larger birds and animals than a stoat.

One final invisible predator which is often overlooked, and only really applicable to those who hope to rear duck, is the pike. Most local people have a fair knowledge of what fish are around where. If the local angling club put two big pike into a particular gravel pit some years ago, they are, like as not, still there. Where pike exist in numbers, the breeding success rate of wild mallard falls to zero. By the time they are eight weeks old mallard are proof against run of the mill pike; if in doubt they should not be put out on suspect water until this age. Really big pike, say, twenty-five pounds and upwards, can take full grown duck if they please. In practice they tend to specialize in snatching wounded birds, on shoot days.

In summary, if the shoot manager wants to see good sport at a reasonable price, he must get someone to control predators. Those responsible for shoots who ignore predator control, and merely release enhanced numbers of birds, on the basis that enough will survive, are being foolish and wasteful.

10 : Costs and Revenue

The costs of running a shoot follow a pattern not unlike most other businesses. A number of costs are fixed, a number are variable, a whole lot more fall somewhere in between.

Whether a shoot rears one bird or one thousand birds, fixed costs stay the same. Variable costs increase pro rata, according to how much shooting, rearing, feeding, vermin control and the like, take place. A thousand pheasants in a wood eat twice as much corn as five hundred birds; two thousand eat twice as much as one thousand. Feed costs increase in a steady upward line.

In between fixed costs and the truly variable costs of running a shoot, is a significant grey area. Most of the costs here tend to increase in steps. At risk of seriously distressing all accountants, these might be called 'semi-fixed' costs.

A prime fixed cost will be rent. Those who take sporting rights over a tract of land expect to pay for that privilege. However, many first time shoot managers fail to appreciate that, behind the substance of sporting rent, lurks the spectre of sporting rates which can amount to several thousand pounds per annum, a most undesirable and unexpected extra cost. To the question: 'What can be done to keep this spectre at bay?', the answer is: 'Quite a lot'.

Some commercial shoots are presently expected to pay sporting rates, others are not and the situation is far from clear. The legal rights of local authorities to levy sporting rates seems to be debatable. Where presently charged, sporting rates are payable at 'so much' in the pound on the rateable value of the hereditament. There are differences in law between England Wales, on the one hand, and Scotland on the other. There are also considerable variances in local authority attitudes to the subject. In those parts where large sporting estates are run on commercial lines, and where high rents are involved, local authorities tend to be keen to charge sporting rates. Other local authorities may be more *laissez faire*. The Scottish Landowners Federation considers that sporting rights are more readily rated in their country than in England and Wales. Shoot managers in East Anglia and some other parts of Southern/Central England, might disagree.

The rights of local authorities in England and Wales to charge sporting rates seem dependent upon interpretations of the Landlord and Tenant Act 1954, Part II, and on the Local Government Finance Act 1988. Shoot managers presently charged sporting rates and those threatened by the spectre, are well advised to consult a bright lawyer. The Country Landowners Association in London produce a booklet on non domestic rating (R1/89) which is useful reading for those subject to the laws of England and Wales; the Scottish Landowners Federation are knowledgeable regarding Scottish law. As an alternative to challenging legality of sporting rates, a shoot manager may opt to avoid – but not evade – such charges.

One avenue worth exploring involves the shooting agreement. If this is drawn up as a licence to shoot, not as a sporting lease, then the shoot manager becomes a licensee as opposed to a lessee. The former is not liable for sporting rates, the latter may be. Such moves however are not without drawbacks. Were something untoward to happen, such as a compulsory purchase of land, the licensee would have no effective rights whereas a lessee would be compensatable. Whether this justifies the shoot paying out thousands of pounds in sporting rates for which it gets zero in return, is a matter for each shoot manager and/or his syndicate, to review.

Before any sporting agreement is signed, there is always a fair element of hassle and wrangle. An agreement will be in force for three, five or whatever years and opposing sides both want to protect their position. Obligations and/or fringe benefits seem undesirable or congenial, dependent upon which side of the negotiation table one sits. When the small print is agreed, a document can be signed.

When sporting rights are in hand and the landowner is his own shoot manager, an awareness of the open market value of that shooting is necessary. Unless a figure approximating to this is built into the shoot manager's costings, he will not have an effective yardstick by which to measure his performance.

Insurance may not be obligatory, however it should be considered a fixed cost by the wise shoot manager.

As already mentioned, truly variable costs include feedstuffs – the more birds you feed the more it costs. Where rearing is concerned, bottled gas and electricity for brooders and heaters is also closely linked to the number of birds involved. The costs of beaters and pickers up is directly linked to how often one shoots. There is no easy correlation between the size of shoot and the fuel consumption of shoot vehicles.

The cost of gamekeepers is a semi-fixed cost of classic dimensions which goes up in big steps. At the lower end of the shooting scale, no keeper is needed; increase numbers and a full time man is needed, further increase numbers and a second and perhaps third keeper are necessary.

The main costs of employing each gamekeeper include: wages, National Insurance, housing expenses, vehicle costs and telephone rental. Secondary expenses cover keeper suits (probably one a year), traps, wires, cartridges, and dog allowances. On top of these a keeper with creative ability will conjure up all sorts of extras, starting with a poultry allowance, to keep those broody hens which he may need in spring (and whose eggs his family will eat all year).

The cost of shoot vehicles warrants special mention. Gamekeepers are notoriously harsh on machinery in general and vehicles in particular. Shoot vehicles get damaged and depreciated infinitely more rapidly than those in general agricultural or forestry activities. It has been said that only test drivers at the Land Rover works, and British gamekeepers, are hell bent on proving that four wheel drive vehicles *will* go anywhere. A vehicle costs the shoot infinitely more when it only lasts two years, than when it keeps going for six seasons. On a marshland shoot in France, no cross country vehicles, as such, were provided. Keepers each had a light van with front wheel drive. Because they knew they could not power through deep mud, no one tried. Keepers skirted around difficult terrain, or occasionally actually walked a short way to fill up feed hoppers or whatever. If these vans got stuck one man could usually lift the front wheels onto dry ground, and off they went again.

Even better than light vans as gamekeeper workhorses, are four wheel, all-terrain motorcycles. Within a decade, these remarkable go-anywhere machines have changed the lives of hill farmers in many parts of Britain. With a sheepdog sitting in the front basket and a bag of feed or bale of hay on the back carrier, these vehicles skim up and down hills, quickly, easily and with no wheel ruts or land damage. Upland gamekeeprs have not been slow to appreciate the advantages of such vehicles. With a gun slung on their back they see more, hear more and can react faster to whatever happens about them, than a man in a conventional vehicle. All-terrain motorbikes often tow a small trailer which is capable of carrying half a dozen bags of feed or four bales of straw over the same terrain as the bike crosses unencumbered.

Some heavyweight load conveying capability is necessary on most shoots. Farm tractors work all right, but do not thrive on mechanical abuse. The most effective vehicle to complement a keeper's small van or all-terrain bike, is a none-too-young middle sized van. Those of the Ford Transit, Sherpa, Bedford variety are not expensive and fit the bill admirably. In summer, when the ground is firm, they can travel anywhere, carrying poults in crates to release pens, aviary sections, bales of straw for feed rides, corn for hoppers and the like. In winter they will need to be kept on firmer tracks or public roads. They do however make excellent beater transport vehicles – able to keep up with a team of guns which moves quickly in Range Rovers or similar vehicles.

A shoot manager will sometimes find himself taking over land on which formal shooting lapsed years previously. It is important, at such times, not to underestimate the cost and time needed to establish a basic shoot infrastructure. The plan may be to shoot pheasants in the woods, duck around the lake, and have a few grouse drives on the small hill – it can probably all be done. But first you may have to build release pens in the woods, duck hides around the lake, and butts on the hill. That means sweat, toil, time and costs. Before undertaking such work, on what is probably someone else's land, the shoot manager needs to ensure that his rights to shoot there will be unchallenged for an adequate period of time. If the shooting agreement is not renewed, the boat can be hauled off the lake in five years' time and moved elsewhere. Most other things tend to stay behind, a bonus to an incoming shoot manager.

Arranging water supplies to new pens and/or rearing areas may not seem difficult or expensive: it can be both. Game strips are more expensive to get established than is sometimes appreciated. In a few cases, small print in the shooting licence specifies that the shoot will be given a set number of game strips each year, as part of the shoot support package. In most cases the shoot manager has to negotiate with a land agent and/or tenant farmers for the acreage he wants. Those who give up land have to be compensated for loss of agricultural income from that land. Cultivation of game strip sites, their planting and fertilizing, involves a series of fiddly little jobs and such work is not relished by most farmers or agricultural contractors.

Game Conservancy cost analysis figures were alluded to earlier when rearing was discussed. Such figures are highly relevant to all who manage shooting or, indeed, carry a gun in a commercial shoot. Figures for the season 1988–89, show that a minority of shoots in the Game Conservancy sample were generating sport at nearly five pounds per bird shot, *less* than the sample average. Relate this to a one thousand bird shot syndicate: it equates to a potential saving of perhaps £500 per syndicated gun per season. Hardly chicken feed, by most standards!

An example of Game Conservancy cost analysis material is shown in the Appendix. Their Advisory Department at Fordingbridge in Hampshire, are usually most helpful when similar material is requested.

However carefully a shoot manager tries to monitor and control costs, all sorts of miscellaneous expenditure seems to slip through the net. A bottle of whisky for the farmer who put the keeper's Land Rover back on its wheels when it slid sideways into that stream, chocolates for the old lady whose cat got run over by the keeper, dinner for the shoot neighbour who was aggrieved by some boundary incursion, and so on.

Most shoot managers give keepers a petty cash float, and agreed discretionary limits for spending which can work well. Petrol and diesel fuel costs however are best kept out of the petty cash system. An account with an honest local garage is one solution. As a routine management control, a shoot managers should, from time to time, check the apparent fuel consumption of shoot vehicles. The mere knowledge that such checks are routine, is usually enough to keep petrol and diesel 'fiddles' within acceptable bounds.

As a counterbalance to all this cash outlay, a shoot can normally expect income from internal and external sources. Internally, the sale of surplus laying birds, eggs, chicks or poults is always a possibility. Sometimes, of course, these commodities are used for barter rather than sale. The sale of game after shoot days hardly transforms shoot economics. It is, nevertheless, a helpful source of cash and can go some way towards paying for the next team of beaters, or towards the petty cash float. Game dealers provide a patchy service around the country; some collect promptly and pay good prices, others collect erratically, with prices always on the low side. A shoot manager should personally handle the negotiation of prices for birds sold; the keeper's job is to agree numbers and help load birds.

Week by week, the shoot manager must be aware of how game bird prices are moving on the open market. All who fail to keep abreast of such matters are in danger of having the wool pulled over their eyes by an opportunist game dealer. The latter, incidentally, are no strangers to 'kick backs' and other incentives to gamekeepers. These may not be in the best interests of the shoot and shoot managers should be aware of, but not paranoid about, such risks.

It is not unknown for game dealers in a given locality to operate a price ring. If this is in line with going prices elsewhere, it matters not. If the local price is noticeably out of step, then game should be sold further afield. When several hundred birds are involved, it is not too expensive for the keeper to drive thirty miles or so to an agreed game dealer in a different district. With any luck a syndicate gun or someone else who shoots, can do this chore instead of the keeper.

The main source of external funds to help the shoot keep body and soul together, will usually come from commercially let shoot days, or from syndicate gun subscriptions.

11 : Syndicates and paying guests

Syndication of guns is the backbone of commercial shooting in Britain and is the situation with which a majority of shoot managers deal. It works very well.

A new shooting year is born each February. Where syndication is the favoured format, it is now that all key decisions are taken regarding the programme for the coming year, also who will shoot as a member of that syndicate.

When new syndicates are established, it is commonplace for prospective members to exceed available places. At such times the shoot manager tends to get cast in the role of 'golf club secretary', with responsibility for vetting applicants. In this rather unenviable position, efforts have to be made to end up with a relatively homogeneous group, who are responsible and safe shots, compatible and credit worthy. When nothing but retired bankers and rock musicians flock to join the syndicate, a wise shoot manager takes a view. Like as not, he orients selection in favour of one group or the other.

When a syndicate is already established it only remains to make annual adjustments. There will always be members who wish to scale-up syndicate involvement, others wishing to scale it down, or leave; there is often a waiting list. A shoot manager has to be as fair and open-handed as possible regarding whose friends or associates are invited to fill vacancies.

A well run syndicate can become a very cosy club – and why not? The great advantage of a syndicate is that it provides financial security for the shoot. It underpins any potential loss and greatly helps cash flow during those expensive summer months when rearing is in full swing.

The shoot manager who opts for private shooting or a combination of that and paying guests, may put off for some months the detailed planning and costing of the new season's sport. The syndicate shoot manager has no such luxury, he has to do all his costings at the very outset as upon those depends syndicate subscriptions and charges for guest days. At an early date, syndicate members are advised of the proposed rearing and shooting programme, also the cost per gun. They are usually required to pay half this annual cost on 1 March and the balance on 1 September.

By acting promptly, early in the new shooting year, the shoot manager helps himself in two ways. Firstly he gets front-end cash into the shoot bank account; secondly he forces the hand of those who might otherwise vascillate over their future level of syndicate involvement. The sooner in the year vacancies in a syndicate come to light, the more easily they are filled.

Syndicate membership has a habit of becoming extremely complex. At the outset, it is all very straightforward: an agreed number of guns become full members. Most pay for this in cash, some by putting in sporting rights over tracts of land, or other barter arrangements. Before long, whole guns start to be split into half guns, quarter guns follow not far behind. This opens the flood gates to a series of obscure and convoluted arrangements between syndicate members, as when three people divide two guns between them. A shoot manager who fails to delegate sub division arrangements – who shoots on which days – is letting himself in for a real headache. Unless someone volunteers to act as social secretary for the shoot, this is a matter which should be sorted out between individual guns.

Obvious problems with excessive subdivision of syndicate guns are twofold. Firstly, the fallibility of human memory is such that people make mistakes. It is not so bad when two or more people turn up on a given day, expecting to shoot the same gun, as they can at least take turn and turn about. The real nuisance for a shoot manager is when no one turns up, and he is one gun short for the day. The second problem with multiple subdivision is that it tends to undermine the democratic lines along which most syndicates are run. An eight gun shoot can find itself with as many as twenty people – all positive, confident and forceful – airing views on fundamental strategy decisions. Subdivision of guns must be kept within acceptable bounds, for the benefit of all concerned.

Most syndicates make provision for shoot day guests. A full gun might typically expect to get two guest slots per season, and a half gun, one. The shoot manager can organize such matters in a variety of ways. A logical approach is for one or perhaps two of the allotted guns to be set aside for guests. On a ten gun shoot this means the syndicate actually comprises eight paid up full guns. Some shoot managers arbitrarily allot an appropriate number of guest day slots to each syndicate member; it is up to them to swop and make changes as necessary. Other shoot managers leave open the allocation of specific days and syndicate members bid for dates they want. These are allocated on a first come first served basis.

Some syndicate members usually live within acceptable travelling distance of the shoot which can be a bonus for the shoot manager and keeper alike. During those long busy days of the rearing season, syndicate member volunteers who can be persuaded to help out with time, machinery or muscle power, are a godsend.

A syndicate member has one big advantage over a paying guest: he is able to take a 'total season's view' of events. For this reason when shooting days are curtailed or even cancelled due to atrocious weather conditions, the syndicate man is less stressed than his paying guest brother.

Syndicate members will normally expect to see a balance sheet and profit and loss account at the end of the season. There is often an accountant within the syndicate who can prepare and 'audit' such documents; failing that, a friendly and inexpensive outsider has to be tracked down. The presentation of shoot accounts is often made to coincide with a dinner, party or some other end-of-season social activity. When a syndicate makes a profit it is usually carried forward to the next season; where a loss occurs, a call on members is usually necessary to balance the books. Needless to say such calls are not popular as they tend to reflect badly on the shoot manager, and prompt members to question the arithmetic for the season which lies ahead!

For a shoot manager who actually owns the land, a syndicate approach safeguards him from having to rescue the shoot if unexpected financial crisis strikes. The disadvantage of syndicates is that it can make private days of shooting difficult. This however seems a small price to pay for financial security. In most cases it is possible for such shoot managers to negotiate with, and buy from the syndicate, one or two private days at a going commercial rate.

Paying guests play a secondary but important role in the British shooting scene. The usual procedure here is for shooting to be let to a whole team of guns, on a day-by-day basis. Most paying guest parties comprise friends and associates who form themselves into a group; sometimes a shoot manager creates 'one-off' parties by pulling together assorted individuals.

The marketing of good quality shooting to paying guests of the right type is harder than it seems. Those who buy shooting are not unlike buyers of skiing holidays or performance motor cars: their hobby is expensive, they afford it, they are discerning and they are cautious. They want to know exactly what they are getting before committing cash.

The shoot owner or manager trying to sell days of shooting may be excused if he plays up the good points and plays down the bad. If the rearing programme is extensive and bags impressive, but the whole shoot is flat as a board with few trees or cover of any type, he may not dwell too much on the quality of birds shown. All too often this leads to unhappiness on the day. Any hope of an ongoing relationships between paying guests and shoot goes out of the window.

Enter sporting agents. These are the firms or individuals who find clients for shoots, and shooting for clients. They have been around for ages, but their ranks have swelled noticeably in recent years. The sporting agent 'earns his corn' by being an honest broker and a market place at one and the same time. The better operators visit the shoot, walk the ground and get a view of what it will look like in midwinter. The fact that it is one mile from the east coast and liable to freezing Arctic winds is of no relevance so long as a party who plan to shoot cock pheasants in January know what to expect. The price they will be paying probably reflects that weather risk anyway.

The shoot manager is always worried in case the proposed party turn out to be a dangerous crowd of novices. When matching buyer with seller, the sporting agent puts his reputation on the line. If his judgement is wrong he gets flak from both sides. The shoot manager will not use him again, paying guests think he is a charlatan. Neither reaction is conducive to future sporting agency business.

Estates which have been selling good shooting for some time have usually learned how to overcome marketing problems. They have a reputation that is well established and a regular group of paying guests. Fitting people into the available programme is not always easy as key dates always seem to get over-subscribed. However, such difficulties are relatively minor compared with actually finding new paying guests.

Shoots relatively new to the game and interested in paying guest guns, will find that a reputable sporting agent can be a good idea. If he brings in business, he is worth his commission. But a shoot manager must strive to do some of his own marketing: don't be entirely dependent on one man or one firm for shooting contacts.

The shoot manager who opts to follow the paying guest road, takes risks which his syndicate counterpart avoids. If the paying guest shoot is unable to fill all available days of shooting, who meets the cash shortfall at the end of the year?

For the shoot manager with his own sporting rights in hand, paying guests are a great idea. Two, four, six or whatever days a year let in this manner can recoup a not unreasonable percentage of a whole year's operating costs. Paying guests are birds of passage, here today and gone tomorrow. Like those travelling goshawks, however, they will be back next year if a local experience is favourable.

Far too many shoot managers fail to appreciate this potential for year on year business. Dealing with paying guest shoot parties, they tend to become greedy and avaricious, guests are not impressed and don't come back. With paying guests, some problems occur as a result of too few birds; even more problems arise as a result of too many birds. The key to success with paying guests guns is – get the numbers right.

Undershooting typically occurs when the weather is adverse, the team of guns shoot atrociously or when there is too little stock on the ground. Not too much can be done about the first two. With the third, a shoot manager will usually know in advance that number problems lurk in the wings, waiting to take centre stage. If there is a chronic shortage of birds, he should cancel the day and refund the paying guest party in full. As an alternative he may be able to 'buy in' some adjacent shooting to make up numbers. In either case the party must be told of the arrangement at least two weeks before the shoot. When there are prospects of a minor shortfall in numbers, the incoming party should again be warned well in advance. An offer of possible compensation or reimbursement of monies already paid, given the worst possible scenario, is a shrewd public relations move. What really causes aggravation is when a party turns up expecting to shoot two hundred head, and learns on the day that they will be lucky to get one hundred. The balance between expectation and realisation is a sensitive one and the shoot manager who is honest and reasonable before crisis strikes wins every time. His paying guests also come back.

Perversely, overshooting often causes more ill will and bad blood than under-shooting. The dragon's teeth of discontent are sown at shoot party agreement stage. Far too many shoot managers lack confidence in their ability to control numbers on shoot days and because of this, they insist on overshoot clauses – usually to the effect that all birds shot over the agreed number will be paid for at a fixed rate. On a sunny day in autumn, when the leader of the paying guests agrees to such terms, this does not look too heinous. On a wet winter's afternoon at 5.00 p.m. it looks different.

Once the shoot manager knows that he has safety net beneath him, and will get paid regardless, he all too often makes no real effort to control numbers. As the day progresses it becomes apparent to the team of guns that an overshoot is likely. At this stage some guns start to exercise contraint; they don't want to be lumbered with extra charges so they pick their shots with care. High birds get taken, others left to fly another day. Other guns may shoot on regardless.

When overshoot charges duly get calculated, the team leader has no real choice but divide that sum evenly between all present. Half his party are then disgruntled, feeling penalized for the lack of self constraint by others. Extracting a hundred pounds or so from all and sundry is not an enjoyable task. The shoot manager gets his overshoot cash but the day ends on a sour note.

If shoot managers ran shooting days efficiently, replacing lacklustre, desultory control over numbers with better management, such problems would not occur. With pheasant shooting, they should have the self-confidence to drop overshoot charges. Sporting agents who condone such charges should think again.

When marketing his shooting to overseas paying guests, the shoot manager is likely to come across Continental, Scandinavian and North American hunting agencies. The range of services offered by some of these is quite exceptional: the game shot can opt for doves in Mexico, geese in Argentina, or jungle fowl in Asia, as well as more conventional partridge in Spain and pheasants in Eastern Europe. The rifle shot, tired of stags in Scotland, may opt for grizzly bear in Alaska, chamoix in Austria, elk in Sweden or a full scale hunting safari in Africa. Most of these overseas sporting agents are totally reliable, a few are not. If the shoot manager does not relish chasing around the law courts of Denmark, Germany and the USA for his money, he must ensure all foreign currency payments are cleared through his bank well before shooting takes place.

Tales of dangerous, ill-mannered, unruly and generally awful shooting behaviour are not uncommon. Members of junket shooting parties seem involved in many such incidents. The shooting junket is an occasion where benign organisations choose to reward senior personnel with several days shooting. Even as the party gathers, its members are clearly different from the norm: some are distinctly inexperienced in all aspects of shooting. It will be discovered next day that British bird recognition is not a strong subject. As he braces himself for the ordeal, the shoot manager must give an especially stern safety talk. This also bears repeating immediately after lunch.

Shooting junkets are not confined to capitalist societies. Politburo and other members of the Soviet hierarchy have huge shooting junkets at former Czarist hunting lodges. Nearer home, the communist mayor of a left wing dominated French city was very partial to shooting junkets. His team of guns would typically comprise the city's chief medical officer, chief architect, chief engineer, police chief and so on, together with a bevvy of wives and mistresses and a grateful city council picked up the bill. Monsieur le Mayor was a nice old gentleman but his party were a shoot manager's nightmare.

Shooting days would be punctuated by unusual incidents, often hair-raising. Guns are lined up forty yards back from a mature wood, birds are expected to cross the valley to another wood. Monsieur le Mayor is somewhere in the middle of the line; on the next peg is his understudy mistress – who fiddled the draw to get that position. At an early stage a woodcock breaks cover: it sees guns and turns back. Well shot by Monsieur le Mayor, it drops into the wood.

With cries of 'becasse', understudy mistress rushes forward from her peg and plunges into the wood trying to find the bird. Noisely, she thrashes about in the undergrowth, using her loaded gun like a golf club. A large number of pheasants have, by this time, moved forward ahead of the beater and lurk in the fringes of the wood, undecided where to go. Unexpected human company in their midst, resolves the dilemma and with a roar of wings they depart en masse, back down the wood. Keepers shout and beaters curse, but all to no avail.

Our heroine now finds the woodcock and rushes back to Monsieur le Mayor. Still clutching her leaf-spattered gun, she thrusts the woodcock at him and embraces him. At that moment he is about to shoot one last pheasant, which actually chose to fly forward not back. The amorous assault knocks him off balance – he nearly shoots his neighbour.

Moral for shoot managers given the prospect of a junket shooting party, look this apparent 'gift horse' very carefully in the mouth.

Dangerous shooting and unsafe gun handling are problems which come the way of most shoot managers, sooner or later. Few individuals survive long enough to compile a meaningful thesis on why and when people shoot dangerously. Over a number of years the manager of a commercial shoot is likely to get more practical experience of the problem than most. As with motoring accidents, inexperience, fatigue and/or alcohol all shorten the odds on a shooting incident occurring. An observant shoot manager must be aware of the danger signs, and try to head off trouble before it occurs.

Shooting guests who are plainly inexperienced are relatively few, but they can be a nuisance and a danger to others. A good solution here is to give them a 'loader'. This person has to be mature and experienced but not necessarily skilled at loading. His job is to carry the guest's gun, hand it to him when it is safe to shoot, also to physically intervene if the gun looks like swinging in the wrong direction. It is the person who, out of the blue, swings through the line or takes a low snap shot straight towards the beaters, whose actions are so hard to foresee.

It has been said that accident prone motorists not infrequently have a flawed crisis reaction. Under normal conditions they drive carefully and competently but under stress or stimulus they are prone to judgemental error – they overbrake, oversteer, go too fast for road conditions, or whatever. It is interesting to ponder that dangerous shots may have a similarly flawed crisis reaction. That thought, however, does not help the man who finds himself looking down his neighbour's gun barrel. Shooting accidents can happen like this: a partridge drive is virtually over; guns are behind hessian butts on a stubble field; directly in front the beaters are coming to the edge of a field of roots. From the last few feet of drive, a solitary partridge jumps up and flies forward, directly at the shoot manager. With beaters milling about, any shot in front is out of the question; the shoot manager half turns to take a shot behind when out of the corner of his eye, he suddenly sees that his neighbour has a gun mounted at that solitary bird, and is about to swing through the line. The shoot manager throws himself flat, shot rips through the top of his hessian butt, and hits the next gun down the line. Fortunately he too anticipated what was about to happen, ducked down and turned his back to the incoming shot. Pellets penetrate his jacket, but no serious damage is done.

Accidents also happen like this: two guns stand facing a great tract of kale; they are sixty yards apart on a stony farm track. A distant cry of 'fox forward' precedes the sudden appearance of the beast as midway between the two it bounds over the track. Both guns fire at the same time, the fox bounds away, two guns reel to the ground. Each has been hit in the face and neck by pellets and stone fragments from the other's ricochet.

Shooting accidents happen in the twinkling of an eye. In the partridge case no lasting damage was done. The fox shooters were both hospitalised; one will carry several shot pellets in the base of his skull till his dying day. In similar cases, people get blinded, maimed or killed.

What can be done about accidents? The first line of defence is vigilance. This is primarily a shoot manager problem, but everyone in the gun line has a role to play: each should ensure that his gun handling and shooting is beyond reproach. Should it be felt that a neighbour is less aware of safety than is desirable, this should be mentioned to the host or shoot manager. At the first available opportunity thereafter, that individual calls all guns together and repeats his safety warning of that morning. Particular reference is made to the type of incident noticed by the worried gun. No fingers are pointed and no names mentioned, those involved get the message. Where keepers, beaters or pickers-up get involved in near-miss situations, the shoot manager should be similarly advised by his keeper, who should say which gun was involved. A similar safety talk may be necessary.

The carrying of guns between drives in wet weather can cause safety problems. Some people become paranoid about rainwater getting into their gun action. To prevent this they refuse to carry it open over the arm, or over the shoulder with the barrels upward. Unless they have, or can borrow, a gun sleeve, some such individuals may find themselves sitting in a vehicle until the rain stops.

Where safety is concerned a shoot manager must not compromise. The sensitivities and whims of individuals take second place. The partridge man was sent home. An emotionally charged scene took place before he left: the shooter was shocked by what he had done; the victim was shocked by being peppered; the shoot manager was shaken by his narrow escape; the syndicate gun, whose guest did the shooting, was chronically embarrassed. That particular day's shooting continued but, in sombre mood. The fox shooters would have been sent home. With their hospitalisation, that day's shooting was abandoned.

For a shoot manager, the three main options – syndication, paying guests, and private shooting – are not mutually exclusive. Some blend quite harmoniously, some do not. In broad terms, most forms of commercial shooting can be made compatible. Private shooting is compatible with paying guest days, but not with syndicates. Non paying guests of the 'estate gun' type are incompatible with all forms of commercial shooting.

Where different forms of commercial shooting are to share the same ground, the only real question is: who gets what, for how much? Once this is agreed, the battle is virtually won. Power sharing, or 'dividing of the shoot cake' between a syndicate and paying guests, works best when one side is clearly 'the rich man in his castle' and the other 'the poor man at his gate'. (We make no apology for quoting from this particular verse of 'All things bright and beautiful'. The fact that modern clerics studiously omit it from the singing, has nothing to do with game shooting!)

When a syndicate is 'in the castle', they control and shoot the centre ground; they dominate the shooting scene. From this position of strength, it is not uncommon for peripheral parts of the shoot to be neglected. Where the shoot programme calls for even a modest hundred pheasants a day, this still represents an average of about fourteen birds per drive. To put this number into the bag, a shoot manager probably needs some thirty or forty birds in each drive. Given this arithmetic, it does not make commercial sense to employ a full team of beaters to drive an assortment of pit holes, double hedges, small spinneys and disused railway lines. However the shoot manager and his keeper both know there are a dozen or so resident birds in each place. Unless they can be blanked into a major drive, these pheasants often have a quiet and uneventful shooting season.

It does make commercial sense to allow paying guests 'at the gate' to walk up these fringe areas of the shoot. Three or four such guns, accompanied by a keeper, can have a splendid day, without setting foot in or near a main drive covert. Furthermore, there is usually no shortage of people prepared to pay good money for the chance to shoot twenty or so head of walked up-game. The syndicate gains unexpected cash and a few birds for the game dealer; with luck some outlying pheasants return to the main woods; the keeper gains tips and he may also sell that hysterical spaniel to an unwary paying guest. Everyone is happy.

A role reversal with paying guest's in the castle and a syndicate 'at the gate' can work. It tends to be successful, however, only where a distinctly big number shoot occupies the centre ground. Most syndicates want at least one hundred birds per day. 'At the gate' shooting usually represents lesser numbers. The owner of sporting rights who lets the shoot to a syndicate, can as an alternative to driven days, buy 'at the gate' shooting from the syndicate.

Private shooting and paying guest days can be perfectly compatible. The shoot manager decides how many days he wants to sell and via his own initiative or helped by a sporting agent, appropriate clients are found. Problems are inclined to occur when paying guests and private guests get mixed together in the same shooting party. Private guests do not mind in the slightest but for reasons which are socially complex and difficult to analyse – paying guests do mind. The shoot manager who wants to see those paying guests come back next year, makes every effort to see that they shoot with fellow paying guests. Guest problems do not occur with those who come along on syndicate days. They are, after all, a form of paying guest, even if a kindly member of the syndicate happens to be picking up their bill.

The *bête noir* of all commercial shooting is the estate gun or obligatory guest. A time was when those negotiating to let sporting rights went to great lengths to retain one or two guns for the Laird or the Estate. The usual ploy by Factor, Land Agent or whatever, was to suggest a ten or twenty per cent reduction in annual rent in return for the estate being able to carry one or two guns on all shooting days. Unwary, inexperienced and unfortunate shoot managers sometimes agreed.

The annual value of a free gun in a commercial shoot equates not to the ground rent but to the total operational budget: keepers' salaries, rearing, feeding and the like, plus ground rent, all divided by the number of guns. In any medium to large shoot, the ground rent is probably around ten per cent of total annual cost: the Land Agent knows this, the shoot manager may not. Proposals to marginally reduce the rent in return for free guns, is tantamount to highway robbery. In any case, the concept of having one or more estate guns imposed on a lowland commercial shoot, is very close to unacceptable.

Estate guns dilute the shooting of those who pay their way as syndicate members or paying guests. People are very sensitive to the rules of fair play. When eight syndicate guns turn up expecting a two hundred bird day, they expect that number to fall to their eight guns. If two outsiders are imposed upon the party, charming and loveable people though they may be, and the party collectively shoot two hundred birds, the syndicate members feel swindled. Those two estate guns between them shot thirty or forty birds, that would otherwise have fallen to syndicate guns; the shoot manager has to increase numbers to around two hundred and fifty before those who pay feel happy. The same thing happens all season; whatever estate guns shoot does not count towards syndicate or paying guns' daily totals – leastwise so far as they are concerned.

The shoot manager groans with despair at the cross he has to bear and rues the day he agreed to allow estate guns. Worse is to follow. The estate owner goes away, becomes ill or grows disenchanted with a difficult shoot day atmosphere which his presence generates. He feels disinclined to 'waste' the two guns his Land Agent so successfully negotiated on his behalf so he starts to send along a succession of butchers, bakers, and candlestick makers, to shoot the estate guns. Since few of these are friends, the landowner makes them pay him for the days they shoot. There then develops a two tier system of payment: syndicate members or paying guests pay full price; estate guns pay the equivalent of airline ticket 'bucket shop' prices. Resentment of these outsiders heightens as the season progresses. The shoot manager finds that in addition to running a shoot, he now has a United Nations peace keeping role, within each shoot day party.

Only in the rarest of circumstances should a shoot manager agree to estate guns. During initial negotiations a Land Agent, Factor or estate owner may *insist* that estate guns be part of the deal. When this happens, the wise shoot manager gathers up his papers and walks away. There is quite enough hassle and stress concerned with running a shoot without this complication.

Opportunities for shoots of all types to generate paying guest income are not limited to pheasant, partridge, duck and grouse. Hares are a highly rated game species in Denmark, Holland, Belgium and West Germany and wood pigeons are also considered sporting. Any shoot with a passable stock of the former, and one or two of those dark fir woods, where winter pigeons roost in numbers, can sell hare and pigeon shoots which take place in February or early March. The format is similar to 'at the gate' shooting, as described earlier; the shoot manager has no need to get involved, other than to negotiate terms and bank the cash. A gamekeeper is put in charge of whatever number come shooting. They walk up hares all morning and for a bit of the afternoon; guns are then placed in, or around suitable pigeon roosting woods and they shoot until dark. Continentals with access to North Sea car ferries are obvious clients, with English east coast the preferred location. 'Home grown' paying guests will, however, buy the hare and pigeon shoot package.

Geese exert a considerable hold on the imagination of those who shoot them, and they attract many who have never previously had the chance. Any shoot manager who has grey geese or Canada geese on his land, should find some way of involving them in the shoot programme. A day shooting pheasants is a day shooting pheasants; precede that with a dawn foray after geese, followed by hot breakfast in a Lodge or pub, and that day becomes a real adventure. As sporting agents will confirm, prospects of a few geese makes pheasant shooting much easier to sell.

Snipe and woodcock, blackgame and capercaille are all exciting species in their own right. Shoot managers lucky enough to have them should make a feature of the fact when marketing their more conventional shooting. Driving pine forest for capercaille or walking bogs for snipe, are occasions when unscripted, unusual and totally unexpected things can happen. Their inclusion in a day's shooting adds stimulus.

Roebuck are a sporting resource not always fully appreciated on lowland pheasant shoots. Roe stalking is a cult activity with Germans among its greatest enthusiasts. In most parts of Continental Europe, this branch of stalking is both expensive and oversubscribed. Good trophy heads are increasingly scarce as buck get slain before their prime.

As with stags, roe antlers or 'horns' are awarded trophy points on an internationally approved scale. Length, weight and dimensions at various places all go into the calculation. Bronze, silver and gold medal heads, are the covetted ideals.

A typical hunting 'package' comprises a week's stalking and two beast shot per rifle. The hunter keeps the trophies, the shoot keeps the venison and gets paid, the keeper gets a tip.

Shooting times are dawn and dusk. In June, which is a favoured month, this means getting up at around 3.30 a.m. A keeper should accompany the stalkers for their first day, to show the lie of the land. After that, most stalkers prefer to be alone.

One particularly old roebuck with antlers almost certainly up to gold medal standard lived on a pheasant shoot. It was very, very cautious and rarely seen, even by the keeper. It lived in an out-of-the-way wood, with a lake on one side and a great reed bed on the other. During the shooting seasons that wood was driven on several occasions, but the old buck was never seen to bolt. He tucked himself away in a swampy corner, and let the beaters walk past.

At least a dozen stalkers tried for this buck. One highly experienced German came back on successive years, with this beast largely in mind. He got as close as any to securing a notable trophy. At 5.00 a.m. one June morning the old buck was in his rifle sights. The deer was browsing slowly through some saplings, but would shortly be in the open. A shot at this stage could be deflected or shattered by a twig or branch and the beast only wounded so the hunter held his fire. Half a mile away, over the fields, a vehicle appeared, driving along some minor road – probably a cowman on his way to milking. The old buck glanced at the distant vehicle, snorted, wheeled around, and was gone. He is probably still about and enjoying old age.

The message for shoot managers is this: If you think you have good roebuck on the land and are not averse to stalking income, check out the situation.

Tail Feathers

Well run shoots can be a pleasure for all concerned. Badly run shoots can be disagreeable and tedious; they can also be a nightmare for the person in charge.

After a season in the job, the shoot manager is a relative veteran compared with the man who lightheartedly took on that responsibility a year earlier. With the gift of hindsight, he can now review a year's progress: what was achieved, what remains to be done? What proved easy, what proved difficult? Which assessments and actions were right, which were wrong? Where was time and money well spent, where it was wasted?

As he looks ahead to a new season, the shoot manager could do worse than remember this: the more time, effort and resources are allocated to achieving the possible, and the less he struggles and frets to achieve the near impossible, the happier he, and those who shoot with him, are likely to be.

Appendix

PHEASANT COST ANALYSIS 1988/1989

INPUTS	AVERAGE COSTS Cost/bird £	PREMIUM COSTS* Cost/bird £
Rent/rates	0.81	0.18
Keepering	5.99	3.44
Equipment	0.54	0.39
Restocking	3.52	2.83
Post release feed	1.86	1.62
Game crops	0.81	0.71
Beaters	1.07	0.65
Total costs	14.60	9.82
Receipts	1.00	1.54
Net costs	13.60	8.28

All costs are in pounds per bird shot.
*Premium costs are the average of the top 25% of the sample.

Source: Game Conservancy Limited, Fordingbridge, Hampshire